EVERYBODY H
THEY GET PUN..... IN THE FACE

A NOTE ON THE TITLE

In October 1987, a 21-year-old Mike Tyson was due to fight Tyrell Biggs to become the Undisputed Heavyweight Champion of the World. In the build-up, Tyrell Biggs had been talking a lot about how he had a plan to beat his opponent. When this was put to Tyson, he replied 'they all have a plan, until they get hit.'

Mike Tyson was a massive inspiration to me growing up. I watched his fights until the videotapes faded away to nothing. When I knew I wanted to write a book about boxing, I knew I wanted to pay homage to Tyson and that iconic moment.

To me it captures the essence of what I think boxing can teach us all. You don't learn what's important when things are going well. It's about how you deal with the punches.

And man Tyson could punch.

EVERYBODY HAS A PLAN UNTIL THEY GET PUNCHED IN THE FACE

12 THINGS BOXING TEACHES YOU ABOUT LIFE

TONY BELLEW

SEVEN DIALS

First published in Great Britain in 2021 by Seven Dials
This paperback edition published in 2022 by Seven Dials,
an imprint of The Orion Publishing Group Ltd
Carmelite House, 50 Victoria Embankment
London EC4Y 0DZ

An Hachette UK Company

1 3 5 7 9 10 8 6 4 2

A CIP catalogue record for this book is
available from the British Library.

ISBN (Mass Market Paperback) 978 1 8418 8471 4

Typeset by Input Data Services Ltd, Somerset

Printed in Great Britain by Clays Ltd, Elcograf S.p.A.

www.orionbooks.co.uk

To my wife Rachael. You're the best of me and the reason
I saw all of my dreams.

CONTENTS

INTRODUCTION

GOODISON PARK, 29 MAY 2016

My nose is the first thing his hand smashes into. The force crunches sickeningly into the cartilage and bone. Then he follows through. Some fighters only punch to score, maybe knock your head back again. Fighters like that are happy to stop at breaking your nose. But Ilunga Makabu punches to hurt you. He knows that when you want to do real damage, you punch right through the target.

The impact of the punch travels down through my face and pushes my jaw back. My legs collapse completely underneath me and I fold down like a deckchair. For a couple of seconds, my thoughts are a jumble of surprise and pain. This is bad. This is very fucking bad. Everything I've dreamed of, everything I've worked for, right out of the window. If I don't get to my feet quickly, the night will be over before it's begun. I'll have been retired by Makabu's left hand. I'm thirty-three years old in the most important fight of my career. My arse hits the floor. The referee starts counting.

'One . . .'

FOUR HOURS EARLIER

Goodison is still quiet when we arrive. There are a few stewards and ticket sellers, a few punters queuing. Its stillness and calm are starkly different to the intensity I feel. The thing that for years I'd predicted would happen is happening. It's happening *now*. Everything rests on whether or not I can beat Ilunga Makabu and seize the vacant WBC Cruiserweight title. What happens in the next few hours will shape the rest of my life. And yet the venue where my future will be decided looks as if it's winding down for the night. We drive past, into the special car park that's normally used by Bill Kenwright, Everton's chairman.

Some fighters are prima donnas – they'll pay other men to carry the stupid collection of Louis Vuitton bags that for them are somehow essential. They start off at the beginning of their careers with a couple of mates helping them and end up with an entourage of twenty-five guys in their dressing room, all claiming they're doing something and all taking a fat wage for doing fucking nothing.

I'm not like that. I've always just turned up with a big, heavy rucksack and then walked into the venue with my boxing kit in my left hand.

Then it happens. I can feel the difference in me as soon as I step onto the tarmac. I've been calm all the way in.

Even while I've been thinking of nothing but the fight, with rap pounding through the car at an unbelievable volume. Aggressive songs. Stuff that I know will provoke me: 50 Cent, Puff Daddy, Wretch 32, Kano. We don't talk, just listen as the bass shakes the car. I try to think as little about my family as I can; they can't have any place in my mind on a night where I know blood is going to be spilled.

Now, I want to hurt everyone. Even the people around me, the people on my side. I want to kill everyone. Nobody's my friend. If anyone gets in my way, I want to damage them, take their head clean off. I don't even want to think about what I'd do if anybody on my team stepped in front of me by mistake. *Mate. You're going to fucking get it.*

I carry on through the stadium I know so well, into the dressing room that means so much to me. It's the place where the first team change and it was the one thing I insisted on. And yet nothing is really sinking in yet. When I'd dreamed about this moment years before, I thought I'd be savouring it all, drinking in the moment, but I'm too angry. Too wired. It isn't about football today, it's about me. It's my face on the posters that are plastered all over the ground.

For a moment my aggression is interrupted by a brief surge of sadness, because I know that if I lose tonight, I won't ever come back here. It's an idea that's been going round and round my head for weeks. I love Everton Football Club. After my wife and kids, it's the most important thing in my life. I've been going to Goodison Park every other

Saturday since I was ten. But if I'm defeated, there's just no way I'll be able to face coming here again. It would hurt too much.

When I enter the dressing room, I spot the man who wraps my hands, Jay Sheldon, laying things out, making sure everything's in order. I look around more and see my coach, Dave Coldwell, who's been at my side for the last three years, and the other members of my tight-knit team: Kerry Kayes, Mick Williamson, my mates Gary and Fran, and my dad. There's just eight of us here in a huge room that's designed for twenty to thirty men. Any noise we make echoes loudly back at us.

I turn to Dave. 'I'm just going to go upstairs and have a look.'

I want to familiarise myself with the surroundings so that when I come out, I'll know what to expect. I don't want any surprises in the crucial seconds before I step into the ring. I also want to have a moment to take in what I've achieved in just getting here.

I've only been nervous before two fights in my life. My first amateur bout, against a lad called Rob Beech. And this one, here. If I lose, I know it's over. I won't get another chance. And there's no way you'll ever see me in the ring again. Since I was fifteen, I've been telling people I'm going to win a world title *here*, at this ground that means so much to me. Even when I was a nobody, a cocky kid in baggy rappers' clothes who'd won nothing, had done nothing, I'd be telling

4

anybody who'd listen what I planned to do. Lots of them laughed in my face. *I'm going to win at Goodison Park.*

We go through the usual pre-match routines – I get my hands wrapped, I fix my low blow – then we reach the moment when normally I'd turn the music up to an obscenely high level. But I've noticed something. I look across to Fran, who's been with me in these moments more times than I can count. I tell him to turn the music off. He looks at me as if to say: *What the fuck? You've never done this before.*

'Trust me,' I say, 'just turn it off.'

There's no way of describing what it's like to hear thousands of people calling your name. But the Everton fans in the Gladwys Street End are singing my name. My fucking name. They're shouting 'Tony, Tony Tony, Tony Tony, Tony, Tony Bellew' – to the tune of 2Unlimited's 'No Limit' – so loud that it makes the dressing room shake.

I turn to Fran, who's standing by the door. We look at each other again.

'I've dreamed of this,' I say. 'I've dreamed of this for so long.'

'Come on, lad. Fucking get on it!'

This is it.

The last twenty minutes fly by so quickly that afterwards, I'll have no memory of any of it until we get the knock on the door from the Sky runner, Ralph.

'Tony, you've got sixty seconds.'

I tell everyone to get out of the room. Then I find the

picture of Rachael and the kids that I've brought with me. The boxer and former footballer Leon McKenzie gave it to me a while ago. Ever since, I've kept it in my gym bag ahead of fights. I stare at the picture for a few seconds, kiss it, then get on my knees.

The room is empty now. I can hear the constant chant of my name and then the swell of excitement as Makabu enters the ring. I'm not a religious person. I don't believe in any divine power; I've seen too much shit to have that sort of faith. But before every fight, I speak to the people I've been close to that I've lost. First, I tell my nan and my grandad not to worry, that I'll get home safe. Then I talk to an ever longer list of people I still care for, even if I can't see them any more.

Last of all, I say a few words to Jimmy Albertina, the coach who changed my life. He's been dead for over ten years, but I've never stopped thinking about him. Not ever. He was a mad Everton fan, too; maybe more than me. I wish more than anything he could be here. Except, of course, in my mind he is.

'Please let me perform,' I say to him. 'You know how hard I've worked. You know what I've done to get here. Just let me perform to the best of my abilities.'

I don't want to be handed the victory. I don't want intervention. All I want is to be able to do everything that I'm capable of. If I'm good enough, I'll win. If I'm not, well, I'll soon find out.'

Then I get up. Time to go to work. I let out one big primal

scream, so loud and fierce that it tears at my throat. 'Come oooooooooon.'

The hairs are standing up on the back of my neck now. Goodison Park is bathed in an eerie blue light. And even over the insane noise that's filling every corner of the stadium, it's possible to pick out Russell Crowe's voice bellowing his character's famous speech from *Gladiator*: 'Are you not entertained? Are you not entertained? Is this not why you are here?' It's followed by the manic screech of an air-raid siren.

I've always known that the public want a bit of entertainment. And I've always been willing to serve it up, whether that's at a press conference or the weigh-in or just before the fight. But I ultimately know that when all that is over, it's time to go to war.

I need that air-raid siren because I want the audience to understand what's about to happen. More importantly, I want Makabu to know what's coming.

Then comes 'Z-Cars', the song that Everton always come out to, which is greeted by an enormous roar. As I walk through the seething crowd, I break into a huge fucking grin. It's like I can't believe that this is happening. I'm so close to achieving everything I've ever dreamed of. It's the best chance I'll get, I know this. Everybody has big moments in their life. Usually you don't realise how significant they are until it's way too late. But I know. I'll never live through a more important night. The song's cymbals are crashing through the stadium's PA system and yet my heart's beating so loudly, I'm surprised that people can't hear it over the music.

All I'm thinking as I approach the ring is: *he cannot hurt me; he cannot hurt me.*

The excited disbelief has worn off now and my body is a mass of nerves. I can feel my heart hammering as if it's trying to escape from my chest. It's up to 160 beats, then 170, rising higher and higher. Nausea slides around my belly and adrenaline rushes around every other part of me. Every couple of seconds I look up and it's almost a shock to remember where I am. I'm scared all over again because I'm at Goodison Park.

I can see the Gladwys Street End. It's completely full. At some point, every single person sitting there lifts their phone to video me as I walk past lights glittering in the air above me. I stop.

'Look at that,' I say, 'that's fucking unbelievable.'

I stand there for two or three seconds, staring. Then I turn my head and see Makabu, already in the ring. He's laughing and smiling. He's cocky. Which is unsurprising, since he's the overwhelming favourite. Most people inside the boxing world think he's going to win and he seems to think so, too. What they've all forgotten is that I've made a career out of upsetting the odds. Proving people wrong has been my speciality.

We touch gloves. I'm watching Makabu, studying all of his body movements. Is he doing anything out of character?

There's no sign of nerves beneath the grin. For a moment I'm disappointed. I want there to be a crack in his armour, something I can exploit. He's in a foreign country with a different climate, I've stuck him in a tiny postbox of a dressing room. He *should* be nervous. He *should* be unsettled, but he's still calm. I can see the sweat beading off him that shows he's warmed up properly. And then I realise that there is something. He believes his own hype. He doesn't think I'm a threat.

Makabu starts the fight slowly, as he always does. Like he's warming up, feeling his way into the contest. Even as my nerves are still firing, my arse twitching, he gives no sign that he's feeling any sort of pressure. There's part of me still telling myself, *he can't hurt you, he can't touch you.* But there's another part that's rubbing up against reality. *This guy knocks other men out cold. Heavyweights, dangerous cruiserweights, former world champions, it doesn't matter – he sends them all to sleep. Over ninety per cent of his victories have been by knockout* – ninety per cent. *He's a wrecking ball.*

I know he's dangerous, I know I'll have to be so switched on, but I don't ever, not for a second, think: *shit, I could lose this.* I have to keep any negative thoughts about defeat out of my mind. If I start to believe I could lose, then it'll make it so much harder to win. That's been another feature of my career: no matter how exhausted I am, or how much punishment I've taken, I'll always think to myself that I've still got that punch that could turn it all round.

I realise that I need to hit him quickly, hard enough that

he starts to respect me and understands that he's in a fight. So I cruise the first round. I'm pinging him with jabs. He's still a slow-moving easy target, so it's boom, boom, boom. Every punch is fast. They're all catching and yet none of them are gaining his respect. Then I hit him on the nose with a straight right hand down the pipe. Fuck off. I can see he's felt it and although it hasn't hurt him, I notice that he's looking at me differently now, like he's thinking, *oh, you've got a bit of a pop on you.*

He gives me a little nod that mixes pain and approval, then smiles at me and plods away. I get him against the ropes again. Another big right hand and then I whack a left hook into his body. He sags. For a second, I even think he's going to go down. Then he makes a noise that only I, in this stadium full of 20,000 fans, can hear. A guttural moan that seems to come from inside his torso.

That's when I think, *I've fucking got ya.* I follow up with a right hand down the pipe and another left hook to the side of his head. A couple of others miss him, going right over his head. But I look in his eyes, which are big and staring, and I can see his mood has changed again. He's thinking, *what the fuck!*

For the first time, he backs up urgently. I've studied him for so long and so closely that I recognise this as an unmistakable sign that I've hurt him. I touch him a few more times and edge him towards the ropes. It's still the first round, but already I'm looking for the finish.

What a fucking stupid thing to do. There's no way you

10

should ever be looking for the finish so early against a man like Ilunga Makabu.

As I back out of the corner after throwing a few more, I make another stupid mistake. I show him my face. He's crouched down in a defensive pose. But then he explodes upwards, throwing a jab that hits me on the chin and knocks my head right back. I should take the punch then slip, staying in range with my hands still up. Instead, like a big dope, I back up with my chin in the air. It's a big easy target. I might as well have wrapped it up and put a label on saying 'open this'. He catches me with his left hand. Just seconds ago I'd been looking forward to victory, now I've just been hit with one of the hardest punches I've ever experienced. Four, maybe five times through my career I've been hurt really badly by punches. This is one of them.

'One.'

My arse hits the floor.

This is bad. This is very fucking bad.

'Two.'

I roll backwards and time seems to freeze.

THE TEN COUNT

Everything that mattered in my life rested on that ten count. My reputation, my financial security, my family's whole future. Literally everything I'd ever done, all the sacrifices I'd made, those horrible long fucking days training

11

so hard that I spewed. All of it came down to one moment on a warm May evening in May 2016. The most dangerous opponent I'd ever faced had caught me with one of the hardest punches I'd ever taken. I'd gone in that ring with a very good plan. In a matter of seconds, Ilunga Makabu had smashed it to pieces.

When you're on your back and all you can hear is the referee counting, you're faced with a decision that only you can make. Nobody can help you. The responsibility sits entirely upon your shoulders. You can sit there, let the referee reach ten and accept that you've lost. That's the easy route. Or you can haul yourself to your feet, put your gloves up and get ready to fight. This way is harder. It means more work, more effort, more pain. But, here's the thing: nobody ever became a world champion by taking the easy way out.

Nothing rips the layers off like boxing. It's the purest test there is. Most sports are team games. In a boxing match it's just you and him. You're on your own. There's no equipment that can improve or hinder your performance: it's a completely level playing field. No teammate to lift you up or drag you down. The only thing that matters is who's worked the hardest. Who's sacrificed more. And, very quickly, the one who's given less gets found out.

That's the first thing I learned about boxing. Everything is up to you. You need the right people around you and you need to listen to people who know more than you do. Whether you aim high or are willing just to be blown this way or that by the wind. Whether you listen to good advice or hang out with fucking clowns. Whether you work hard or waste your talent. Whether you push on, no matter what the circumstances, or quit. Whether you choose to project confidence or give up. Whether you treat learning as a lifelong process or think you know it all. Whether you focus obsessively on your dream or treat it like a hobby you can pick up and put down whenever the mood takes you. Whether you understand that you're responsible for every element of your life or hide behind excuses, telling yourself that everyone else has it easier than you. All that is *your* decision. Nobody else can make you get out of bed or pick yourself up off the canvas. Nobody else can find your motivation. It has to come from you. That can feel like a frightening thought. And yet it's also exhilarating. You can't change the cards life has dealt you, but you can choose how you play them. Everything is up to you.

WHY THE FUCK SHOULD I LISTEN TO YOU?

I never thought I'd write a book. It's just not something that people who come from where I grew up do. I don't have any qualifications. I was expelled from school, for fuck's sake. And I know what my reputation is. Some people see me as aggressive, cocky and loud. I know others see me as a bully. There are days when I can see why they might feel that way about me. I sometimes think that some of the

13

silly shit that comes out of my mouth actually guarantees I can't be clever.

But then I remember that I'm really good at figuring my way out of situations in all different walks of life. That's one of the reasons why I decided that I'd take the plunge and become an author. Over the years, I've had approaches from a number of different publishers. They all wanted to make my childhood and all the shit that happens outside the ring a major part of the book. I didn't want to spend 300 pages discussing stuff that happened when I was a kid. Not because I had a bad upbringing – I didn't. I have two very loving parents who have worked very hard their whole lives. Stuff happened in our family, like it does in thousands of others up and down the country, and I've no interest in dragging it up. I don't want to appear as though I'm playing the victim card.

But what did excite me was the opportunity to pass on some of the things that I've learned from my two decades in the ring. I'm not saying I'm anything special. I'm not a role model and I'm never going to say or do the perfect thing on every occasion. But although I'm only thirty-eight, I feel as if I've been through such a lot in life. I've had hard times, I've done bad things that I'm not proud of, but I've always come out the other end.

I had a good career. I was world champion. I had thirty-four professional bouts and won thirty of them. Twenty times, my opponent hit the canvas. Boxing was everything for me and for many years it was the only thing I knew. But since I've retired, my horizons have grown. I've spent time talking to people from different backgrounds, especially those who have seen combat and battled demons like mine.

I began wanting to understand more about myself, particularly the demons that had sat on my shoulder for years. Going on *SAS: Who Dares Wins* brought all that to a head. Days of physical exhaustion and mental torture culminated in me standing face to face with Ant Middleton, the chief instructor, with every single atom in my body urging me to smash him in the face. He'd pushed me to the absolute limit. I remember the moment he braced, preparing himself for the attack that looked inevitable. I could see his jaw clench and his fists tighten. For three or four seconds, the two routes I could take revolved in my brain: *was I going to smack him? Was I going to let it go?* In the end, the reason I pulled my punches was because everybody thought I'd belt him and I was desperate to show people I could control my temper.

My experiences on that show changed me in so many ways. For the first time in my life, I really looked myself in the eye. This book is part of that work.

What I have realised in the months since is that so much of what I did, most of it by instinct or passed down through generations of fighters and trainers, or because I'd taken the time to work it out for myself, isn't just useful in the ring. It can help anyone. Because whether you're a boxer or a soldier or you work in an office, we've all got the same basic equipment and many of the same principles apply. People talk about a boxer having a heart or spirit, but what they really mean by that is their attitude. How much punishment, how much suffering can they take and keep going? How much work are they willing to put into their training? How many sacrifices are they prepared to make outside the ring?

I got to the top of my profession not because I was more talented or physically gifted than other fighters, but because I worked and thought harder than all of them. I'm living proof that you don't need to be born a genius or an athletic freak of nature to achieve your dreams.

Some people were born world champions. They're so obscenely talented that they glide through life. When you look at them, it's as if they've got an aura. I'm not like that. Photographs of me from school show me looking like an absolute fat balloon. Physically, I'm not a lot different now to how I was then. I always found running hard. And circuits were fucking murder. When I was starting out I used to have to psyche myself up to get on the bus that would take me to my Tuesday gym session. I was never the quickest or the strongest. Far from it. And on top of that, my hands are small and vulnerable; they break easily and often. None of that is very useful for a fighter.

What I do have over everybody else is my attitude, my drive. I've never given up or backed down, no matter what I was going through, no matter how hard things were. Most fighters would reach a point in their training when they'd give up. Me? Never. I don't know what it is that's wrong with me. I won't throw in the towel. No matter how tough the problems I faced, I'd try to figure them out – and I'd keep going and going and going until I had. I knew that all the bullshit, all the excuses, all the justifications melt away when you cross the ropes. If you did the work, if you suffered for what you wanted, you'd feel the benefit. If you cut corners, if you went easy on yourself and rested on your laurels, you'd get found out. Painfully. That's what took me from being a clueless kid who'd been expelled from school to champion of the world.

Your ambitions and life circumstances will be different from mine, but I hope that some of the skills and techniques that helped me to achieve my dreams can help you with yours. I've been in some pretty extreme situations, and yet I think so much of what I've been through and learned is applicable to everybody's day-to-day lives. In this book, I'll talk about the importance of hard work and setting the right goals, how you can build your confidence and strengthen your resilience, and why you should never stop learning. I'll explain why you should never let quitting become a habit, the best way to respond to failure and how crucial it is to surround yourself with good people.

None of what I'm going to tell you is really that unusual. I don't have any magic tricks and most of what I say is common sense. But I have lived it all. I know what it's like to be broke, I know what it's like to have people laugh in your face and I've had to pick myself up again after suffering a humiliating defeat. And yet, there was never a point in my two-decade journey when I ever lost faith in myself. Nothing that anybody could ever say or do could shake that belief.

That's why I also know what it's like to win, to achieve all of my dreams. In this book, I want to help you do the same thing.

A ten count. Ten seconds. Count it out loud now to yourself. Ten seconds to find yourself, find who you are and what you can be. I was able to do it and I want you to know that you can, too.

CHAPTER 1
THE WEIGH-IN

It's the second fight of my amateur career, against a kid called Ryan Connolly at the Heatwave Leisure Centre. All this is still so new and thrilling to me. I love the smells, the sounds, the routines that surround a fight. The raw crackle of excitement I feel down my spine when the bell first goes. I cannot believe that I'm allowed to do this.

After we have our medical, me and some of the other lads who are fighting tonight go down to put our fight gloves on. A couple of younger kids are hanging around with us. When they try their gloves on, I see that they're briefly overcome with nerves.

'Bloody hell,' they say, their voices squeaky with a mix of hormones and anxiety, 'they're thin, aren't they? What happens if I get hit with them?'

I can see that I'm different. I exhale with pleasure when I slip them on.

'This fuckin' fella's had it when I hit him with these,' I say.

The idea that he might hit back barely even occurs to me. Later that evening, I knock Connolly out in twenty-nine seconds. This is the

19

first thing I've ever been really good at. When I go out in the ring, I'm no longer just a tear-arse kid from Wavertree. I'm a fighter.

Where I come from, nobody gives a shit about anything except boxing and football. Nothing else touches the sides. Football comes first – it runs our city. Next up is boxing, and then after that, quite a long distance after, it's clowns and jokers.

In Liverpool, people grow up wanting to be either a fighter or a footballer. When I was a kid, all I wanted was to play once, just once, even if it was five minutes, for Everton Football Club. In hindsight, there was zero chance of that ever happening, which has been a big disappointment to my wife. I could *play*, I just didn't look as if I could. So nobody ever gave me a fair crack.

What I was definitely good at was fighting. For a long time, though, and I don't really know why, the idea that I might become a professional didn't cross my mind. For me, fighting didn't have much to do with putting on a pair of gloves. It was what you did in the streets around where I grew up in Wavertree. Or at school when somebody picked on my younger brother. (Being one of the biggest, heaviest kids in my year was a definite advantage there.) I've never shied away from a fight. In fact, I've been in that many scraps that I can't even remember the first time I threw a punch, or the first time I took one. If you look at it from one angle, you'd say my life has been a big blur of fighting.

None of that was a surprise. Fighting is in my blood.

Dad was a proper fighting man – one of those fellas who seem to spend their whole life brawling. His dad had been a copper, which meant that my dad would get into brawls the second he walked out of his door. With all that going on, it probably wasn't a shock to anybody that he rebelled by doing some very silly things at a very young age and ended up in prison. But in the years that followed, he put all that behind him and managed to build up a successful security business, which allowed him to combine his love for punching other men very fucking hard with earning an honest living. For a long time, he ran the nightclub doors across Liverpool. He was the prick who was telling my friends' dads: 'You're not getting in.' Sometimes he was the one who was giving them a hiding.

Outside of that, he found time to give boxing a go; although he didn't get very far. He won his first bout but then in the second, he got a couple of jabs to the head he didn't like and lost his rag. As soon as the bell went, he raced back to his corner, picked up a stool and chased his opponent. That was the end of his boxing career. He's a very tough man and even now I wouldn't want to get into a tussle with him. But he never had the discipline you need for boxing. He didn't understand the mindset that you sometimes have to get hit in order to get your shots off. His whole attitude was just bang-bang, good night.

Fighting was a way of making him proud of me. If I'd have come home from school with ten GCSEs, he'd have smiled and given me a tenner. If I'd come home and said,

'Dad, I've just broken another kid's nose in a scrap,' he'd have burst with pride and given me whatever I wanted. I know that sounds mad, but that's just the way our family was. I was no different to any young boy: I wanted to impress my dad.

I've always said he was a fantastic father. Unfortunately, he wasn't a very clever husband. Things went wrong and on the day after Boxing Day 1992, when I'd just turned ten, he left home. His departure made him public enemy number one for everybody else in our house, but I still adored him. I understood that he'd been a fucking idiot and yet he was still my dad. There was never any question that we lacked love – my dad wasn't one of those guys who just disappeared; he was always there for us, always provided – and yet his work – on the doors Friday, Saturday, even Sunday nights – restricted the time he could spend with us. And then he went to jail for the second time, when I was still only fourteen. That felt like another kind of heartbreak.

During all this, my mother was a receptionist at the local sports centre. The break-up hit her really hard. Suddenly, she found she was bringing up four boys almost by herself. She ended up working every hour she possibly could. Mum needed the money, but I think it was also a way for her to take her mind off her situation.

As every year went by, she found it easier to cope, but over that same period I began to drift away. By the time I was in my teens, my friends had become my real family. I had about seven or eight close friends growing up. I've still got the same seven or eight close friends now. Most of us were from broken homes. My mum was out most of the day and night, so my house became the place where we'd all hang out. We didn't have to ask permission to do anything because there was nobody to ask. So we'd all just be in my room, door locked, and there'd be murder going on: shouting, bawling, screaming.

I spent the majority of my time at school either pissing around with my mates or playing football. I was a cheeky kid rather than a nasty one, the kind that had an answer for everything. I had massive respect for some teachers. But not all of them. There was a maths teacher who seemed to like degrading me: he told me I wasn't going to do anything because I was weak-minded and I couldn't stick to a task. My PE teacher knew I had physical ability and yet he also claimed I'd never make anything of myself because of my temper. It's been good to prove those fuckers wrong.

Once I'd given up on the idea of playing for Everton, I was left with a vague plan that I'd get the right qualifications to stay on in education. I'd always looked up to my brother Westley, the exceptional one out of all of us, the one with real brains who'd gone to university. And I wanted to do the same. Although it's possible I was more interested in getting on the ale and having a laugh rather than actually studying.

As it happened, I never got to find out. One of the teachers at school had a carton of Ribena smashed in her face by a lad who I already didn't like. I said that what he'd done was out of order. That led to some cross words with one of his mates, whom I liked even less. Which led to me smashing his jaw in and knocking out a fair few of his teeth. I belted him so hard and so often that my right hand was swollen for days after. As I was doing this, he was stabbing me in the head with a compass. The net result was that I got expelled and the other kid didn't, which even now doesn't seem that fair.

Actually, it didn't even end there. There was a flurry of phone calls, people ringing me up saying, 'Do you know who the kid's brothers are?' No, I didn't, and nor did I care, but they obviously didn't know who my dad was, either.

There wasn't much about the situation that bothered me. There was a bit of chivalry about what I'd done – that woman should never have got belted off a young boy – but ultimately, it wasn't my fight to fight. I just wanted to scrap. That was always my problem. My fists were quite good at getting me out of trouble, but they were just as capable of dropping me in the shit.

The mad thing is, after the school expelled me, they called to say that they still wanted me to come in and sit my exams. I think what they were trying to say was something along the lines of: *we think you're a good kid and we liked the way you defended one of our teachers, even if in an ideal world you wouldn't have caused so much damage to another pupil's face and body, so for the sake of appearance we're going to punish you.* Madder still, they then invited me back to take sixth-form physical education. Instead of grabbing this lifeline, I was so pig-headed and angry that I told them to fuck off, which to this day is one of the biggest regrets I have.

So that was that. I was fifteen years old without a single qualification to my name and absolutely no idea what to do with my life. I had no job, I was signing on. All I thought was: *What the fuck have I got?* My mates were starting to work out what they were going to do and I was just a bum on the dole.

I had no real belief in myself and I didn't think that I had much chance of making my way out of my circumstances. Growing up where I did, all I thought was: *I'm just another piece-of-shit kid.* We were treated like we were nothing, little cunts who'd achieved nothing and would go on achieving nothing until we died. That sticks with you. I didn't know anyone who'd made it out of our bit of the city. It seemed *impossible* that a kid from Portman Road in Wavertree could ever become a world champion. Nobody else from my neighbourhood had ever become a world champion. As far as I knew, nobody else from round where I grew up had become wealthy or done anything.

Wavertree is the place that defines who I am. It's the place that made me. Without it, I wouldn't exist. And it'll always be special to me, because I have such amazing memories of my life there. There were rough edges, of course, but the people there are like nobody else on the planet: funny, resilient and kind. There was a brilliant sense of community, with everybody looking out for each other. And when I was a kid there were even things to do. You could play football on the streets or in the Aldi car park for hours at a time. We could go to youth centres, where there were pool tables and table tennis, with amazing people who gave up their evenings to look after a load of tear-arse kids. We used to have five-a-side competitions where we'd fight like fuck just to win a carton of juice. Nearly all of those places are gone now, lost to government cuts. It's no surprise that these children, who have nothing to do, are getting involved with guns and knives and other insanity. I was lucky that I grew up in an environment that was tough but not lethal. And yet for all kinds of reasons, our horizons were limited.

When you're a kid, your heroes should be doctors, lawyers and nurses, but nobody like that lived around us. The people we did see, driving around in boss cars, wearing gold chains and Rolexes, were drug dealers. It was much easier for us to idolise them than surgeons, because we knew them. They lived across the street, they had kickabouts (still wearing their Rolexes) with us, slapped us and told us to behave when we got out of line, and kept us away from any really bad trouble. The people doing professional jobs might have only been across the water, but as far as I was concerned, they might as well have lived on Mars. For lads like me, the street corners felt like the only way out. Especially if you had a taste for the nicer things in life. Which, unfortunately, I did.

What stopped me from doing anything more serious than messing around with it all was my dad. It wasn't really anything he said – it was more the example he set. He always had nice things because his security firm was doing well: a BMW sports car, expensive clothes, numerous houses. That showed me that you could get those items by making money the proper way. He chose to stick to the business he'd built, even though the trade he was in meant that he was surrounded by opportunities to start dealing.

If my dad had been earning his money illegally, there's every chance I'd have followed him. So that's why instead of going out on the streets in a big way, I took a job my mum got me as a lifeguard at the Peter Lloyd Leisure Centre. That gave me the chance to look around a bit and try to work out what it was I wanted to do with my life. For a while I considered joining the navy, because I knew it'd remove me from the sorts of temptations that were everywhere in our neighbourhood. I even passed the entrance test. But around the same time, I decided that I was going to try to make a go of a sport that I'd just started taking seriously: boxing.

I actually tried kick-boxing first. Unfortunately, I knocked a couple of people out with punches, so I got disqualified. Instead, when I was fourteen, I began training at the 051 Club gym with Terry Quinn and Noel Quarless, a former pro boxer who was now working the doors with my dad. They taught me the fundamentals of boxing. To begin with, I was only doing it as a hobby, a good way of having a fight without getting nicked. The idea of being a professional, let alone a world champion, didn't really enter my head.

27

Terry was brilliant – a lovely, lovely man who had a great record in amateur boxing – and he introduced me to proper training. While my dad had shown me the basics of fighting and we'd done some pads in the yard, Terry showed me much more. We did workouts in the sauna, ran up and down the stairs. I learned what it felt like to put your body under extreme amounts of stress. Whatever we did, I'd never shy away from it. I'd be doing exactly the same as the big hard fellas I was training alongside. To begin with I was able to keep up with them, but after a while I started to out-work them.

Those hours spent doing press-ups in the blistering heat of the sauna and killing my legs as I dragged myself up those stairs for what felt like the millionth time in one afternoon were the first indication I had of the hard work that was needed if you wanted to be a decent boxer. Terry was also the first person who spotted I had something. I was there with my dad one day, when he turned to us and said: 'You've got ability. The lad can really box. I know he can. He's got a punch on him.'

That's when my dad took me to my first boxing gym, Kirkdale ABC, which was in an old community centre on Stanley Road. The overpowering memory I have is of sweaty gloves. I did one session, but there was something about the atmosphere that made me feel uncomfortable. I didn't know anybody there and the people weren't anything like me. I couldn't make that connection, so I didn't go back.

I followed that up by going to the famous Rotunda ABC a week later. I did one session there, too. The coach, Jimmy Albertina, asked me if I'd ever boxed before. I said no. He put me on a punching bag. I was moving round the bag like a fucking animal, hosing it with punch after furious punch. Jimmy stopped me and looked me in the eye.

'You've boxed.'

'No,' I said, 'I haven't boxed. I'm telling you, honest to God, I've never had a bout.'

Jimmy wasn't having that. 'The way you move and the way you punch, you've definitely been in a ring before. I don't understand why you're saying you haven't.'

We agreed to disagree and I asked Jimmy the only question that mattered to me: 'All I want to know is: when can I fight?'

Jimmy set me straight. 'Listen, son. You don't tell me when you're going to fight. I tell you. And it's going to be twelve to eighteen months until we put you in the ring.'

As soon as he said that, I walked out and started to talk to Stockbridge ABC. I didn't want to wait. I'm just not somebody who likes to hang around hoping for things to happen; I like to *make* them happen. If you want to get anywhere, you have to create opportunities and take them straight away. More than that, I wanted to test myself. I had to find out whether or not I had the ability to stand there and trade punches. I understood even then that until you've actually put yourself in those situations, you just never know. Not for sure. Within six weeks, I had a match lined up.

Rob Beech was my first amateur opponent. He had a beard on his chin and looked like he had a rug on his chest, whereas I barely had a single hair on my bollocks. My arse was twitching. In the first round he hit me hard, harder than anyone had ever hit me before. Suddenly, I realised that things had got real, very quickly. I remember I could see my dad out of the corner of my eye. That steadied me. I could never spew in front of him. I just wouldn't be able to live with myself if he saw me give up. And then something inside me went: *Right, bite down on your gumshield. Fuck it, let's fight.*

I ended up beating Beech in a third-round stoppage. After that, things suddenly started to move quite quickly. I demolished Ryan Connolly and then found myself in the first round of the Under 10s novice tournament against Ryan Cunliffe from the Wigan ABC at the Montrose Huyton Suite. It was one of those smoke-filled social clubs that you saw everywhere in the amateur game. Kids fighting while old fellas watched, ciggies in hand. Everyone was on the ale and we were just another entertainment. It was all very much, 'Bring out the gladiators.' One night there'd be fighting on the bill, another night it would be an Elvis impersonator.

I went into the match with a bruised rib, although I didn't realise quite how damaged it was. I'd been sparring with an undefeated professional called Gary Lockett who was fighting for the British title and he'd caught me with a left hook on my body, but I thought nothing of it. There was just a really sharp twinge and I said to myself: *that's*

just what happens when you get hit with a really good body shot.
The thing I really took away was that Gary was astounded by how good I was. I was in a ring with a fighter, a real fighter, and I was holding my own. Terry Quinn's praise had stayed with me, but this was the first time that I realised for myself that maybe I could do something.

The fucked rib didn't do much to affect my confidence. I was 2 and 0. Both knockouts. That rarely happened in the amateur game. Actually, it never happened. Cunliffe came out hard. He jabbed my head and then threw a straight right hand to my body. Oh my fucking God. I went back to the corner: 'I think he's broken my rib.' I remember Mark Kinney, my coach at Stockbridge, and Tosh Fielding, his assistant, were in the corner. They lifted my vest and there was a red patch of blood. Tosh looked horrified.

'Stop it! Stop it! Fucking hell. There's blood under his skin!'

I wasn't willing to give in. 'Don't panic,' I mumbled through my mouthguard. 'I'll get him in the next round.'

Tosh was still a bit stunned. 'No, no, you've got to stop.'

Even then I got tunnel vision when I fought. The only thing that mattered to me was winning, nothing else registered. So I didn't acknowledge what Tosh was saying, I just told him to be quiet. I looked Mark in the eyes and said, 'Just give me another round, I'll get rid of him.'

Mark stared back. 'No problem.'

It didn't last long after that. Cunliffe was out cold and I was up on the ropes screaming at everyone. Right from my first days I was loud and out there. The normal protocol in amateur boxing is that when you win, you nod your head to the judges and that's it. You walk out. It's still got a gentlemanly ethos. Whereas I'd knock people out and then even as their head was slamming down onto the canvas, I'd be jumping up onto the ropes or screaming all round the ring, making sure that everyone in that room knew that 'I'm the best amateur boxer that this country has ever seen.'

I was already thinking like a professional, carrying myself like a professional, even though I was fighting amateurs. Strictly speaking, my style wasn't suitable for the game, but those poor fuckers didn't stand a chance.

Slowly, as I trained, my physique changed. That fat kid who loved playing football became longer and leaner. I was learning more about myself, too.

You can't know if you'll go on to become a world champion. There's too much work, dedication and sacrifice involved. But you can find out quite quickly whether or not you've got the kind of spirit that can at least get you started. The first time you're smashed in the face is, for many, that moment.

Those seconds after being hit are sink or swim. It's your chance to say, 'I've had enough, that's it.' And there'd be no shame in that: that's just the way you're wired; everybody's different. So if at that moment you feel a surge of self-pity or are tempted to quit, then let it go straight away. Find another sport.

If, by contrast, you're the kind of person who says, 'I'll have some more of that,' then you might just be the right person for this game. I loved it. I knew that from the second that Rob Beech's fist had crashed into me. I loved the violence and the pain and the rush of excitement that came with fighting. The first time my nose got burst and filled up with blood, all I thought was: *Right, I'm going to get you.* I'd tasted blood, which freaks most people out, and I thought it was nice. Which is a fucked-up thing in itself.

Boxing gave meaning to my life. It was the first thing I'd ever found that gave purpose to both my body and mind. I don't even remember when the thought first came into my head, but suddenly I found that I'd gone from being a lost fucking bum to a kid with an ambition that not only felt big and mad and intimidating, but also *possible*: I wanted to become world champion. And if I couldn't ever play for Everton, I wanted the next best thing: to win that title at Goodison.

FIND YOUR GOALS

Boxing gave me everything. It gave me discipline, it gave me hope, a way out. It gave me my dreams, then helped me to fulfil them. That's why it was so hard when it stopped, because suddenly there was this huge hole in my life.

I was lost after I was expelled from school. I had no idea what I wanted to do and no real idea what I was capable of. Boxing changed all that. That burning desire to become world champion meant that for two decades, I had a long-term goal. And no matter what stage of my career I was at, no matter if I'd just lost a fight, that goal never changed. Over time, as my family grew, I realised that I also wanted to be able to ensure that whatever happened to me, Rachael and the boys' future would be secure, so that became another goal. Family security, money and world titles. I stayed focused on those things.

You won't achieve anything if you don't set goals and they're not working towards something that really matters to you. I fought to provide for my family, but it wasn't the money itself that was important to me, it was what it represented: security. Goals provide both the framework and the motivation you need if you want to get anywhere. When I've set myself a goal, I have purpose and a sense that I'm moving forwards. I feel as if I'm in control of my life. I can't find your purpose for you. I can't make you like getting hit and enjoy the taste of blood. But I'm here to say you do need purpose to get anything done. You need to find your equivalent of walking out at Goodison. You need to work out what you're willing to get punched in the face for and keep going. You don't need to have big skyscraping ambitions. Your goal could just be getting to a stage where you can support your family or owning your own business. And your goals don't need to be professional. They could just be about losing weight and getting fitter or becoming a better husband and father.

It's worth devoting effort to thinking hard about what your goals should be. Sometimes you'll know instantly. Other times, it won't be so obvious. Sit down and try to work out what you'd like to change about your circumstances. What are the things that you've always wanted to do but haven't found the space or time in your life to get started on? What about those little voices at the back of your mind that you've always been too busy to listen to? Maybe you've been wanting to start playing five-a-side football again but you know you're short of fitness and the idea of finding a game feels a bit tough, so you keep putting it off. Or it could be that deep down you know that you're not happy with your job and that you want to be doing something completely different.

Don't be stupid with what you ask of yourself. Don't look to achieve the impossible. Nothing demotivates you like failing to reach a goal, however unrealistic, and nothing motivates you more like hitting one. And it has to be something you want, not something other people want for you. My dad's dream was always to have a kid who could fight like fuck. But if boxing hadn't been something I was obsessed by and I just wanted to live out my father's ambitions for him, there's no way in the world I'd have been able to drag myself through those hard times and early mornings. The more passionate you are about something at the beginning, the more likely you are to be doing it still in a year, two years', three years' time. If you can't see that passion lasting more than a couple of months, then ask yourself whether you should consider following a different path.

The reason this chapter is called 'The Weigh-In' is because, at the end of the day, the scales don't lie. You need to look at yourself with the same dispassionate honesty as those scales. What do you want, how can you get there? What are you good at, what are you bad at? What can you do well? What needs work?

Set realistic goals. Achieve them. And once you've achieved them, you have to set more quickly. The moment I tell myself I've done it all, what then? And sometimes, believe me, those goals will scare you. Like writing a book.

TELL A NEW STORY

When you have a clearly defined ambition, it enables you to look at the world, and yourself, in a different way.

I spent so much of my early life being told I was a waste of space. And there's only so many times you can close your ears before you begin to think: *well, am I?* You end up believing them and it becomes your destiny. *You think I'm filth? Fine, I'll be filth.* Nobody ever encouraged me, nobody ever took the time to point out what I was good at. I had to prove those things to myself.

Boxing offered me a way out of that way of thinking. Once I'd thrown myself behind that dream of becoming world champion, I stopped seeing myself as a failure who was going nowhere and unworthy of anybody's respect. I'd become somebody who was on the road to somewhere. That meant that when I experienced setbacks, I stopped seeing them as failures and started to understand that they were just steps on the path to success. You can't change what happens, but you can change your attitude towards it. And once you realise that, it becomes your greatest power. Everybody has the ability to act as the author of their own story – it's up to you to use it.

What cuts me up is knowing how much potential there is out there for human beings and how much of it goes to waste because people tell others who could accomplish great things that they're worthless. It's not the way it should be but don't let yourself get demoralised by it. Use it as motivation to demonstrate to them that it doesn't matter that they were handed every advantage, you're fucking going to show them what real achievement looks like. And when you make it, it'll feel all the sweeter for it.

MAKE IT SPECIFIC

I don't think I realised it at the time, but I can see now how that specific, measurable ambition – becoming world champion – was probably more valuable than something vaguer like 'I want to be good at boxing.' Where would I have even started with that?

I don't want to sound too cold or scientific about it. And nor do I want to sound too spiritual, either. But there was definitely something about how specific my dream was – that I wanted to win that belt at Goodison Park – that made it feel personal to me. It also helped me to imagine myself getting there. That image was something I could call upon when I was struggling. No matter how horrible those 5 a.m. runs were – and they were almost always fucking horrible – they were always *for* something.

LITTLE STEPS

Everyone has to start somewhere. I didn't become a world-class boxer in one leap. I'd have been absolutely annihilated if I'd climbed into the ring against someone like David Haye in my first fight. To get to that point, I had to take a thousand smaller steps.

I know for a fact that if I'd known how much work and sacrifice would be involved in becoming world champion, I'd have got so overwhelmed that I might never have got going. That's why it was so important that I made a commitment, joined a boxing gym and took that first step. It didn't feel significant at the time, but it meant that the next step was easier, and the step after that, and the step after that. You have to find your way in.

The same is true of any project or ambition. You're not going to be able to run a marathon without doing any preparation, but you can start off by going from the couch to a more manageable 5K. That way, suddenly you'll find that the idea of going further isn't so intimidating. You might want to become a barrister, but there's no way you're going to be able to stand there in court in your big fucking wig unless you've got all the qualifications and experience that the job demands. The idea of all the obstacles you're going to have to overcome in the future could become so overwhelming that it paralyses you. Don't let that happen. All you can do is focus on the things you can do now to get you moving in the right direction.

You have to start somewhere and the first step is always the hardest, but once you've made that first small commitment, everything else will follow.

FIND YOUR MOTIVATION

Nothing's given to you, nothing is easy. Most good things in life come from sacrifice and hard work. In order to reach your goals, you need to find the motivation that will drive you on when times get tough. You need a 'why' as well as a 'what'. There's no point in climbing into the ring and taking punches if you don't know why you're doing it. Otherwise, you're just a fucking madman with a death wish. Once you know why you're opening yourself up to pain and disappointment, then they'll both be easier to bear. I was lucky in many ways, because my workplace gave me a big target to aim for: world champion.

Most boxers come from nothing, like me. They've been starved all their lives, been out on the streets doing nasty things before they got into the ring. They're dealers, pimps, jailbirds. That's why they have that fire in their bellies that makes them want to push and push. There are a very few, like Conor Benn, who have grown up with nice things and gone on to make it. It's rare to come from privilege and be able to go and fight the way he does. But his motivation came in wanting to impress his father.

I didn't come from privilege. The purpose of fighting for me was to escape the place I was born, but in that respect, Conor and I are similar. I loved my dad, but I wanted to show him that I could do stuff he couldn't. Even though he backed me all the way, I still wanted to be better than him or anyone else in my family. I wanted to make my dad proud by becoming a better version of him. And I wanted to give my kids the best life I possibly could. I think all that is perhaps why I was willing to go further than anybody else, because anything was better than the idea of being a failed fighter who'd got stuck in fucking Wavertree.

If your goal is getting a new job, make sure you know what that new job really represents to you, otherwise you're just going to end up chasing an empty shell. Is it because you want a career that challenges you? Or is it just that you want more money to help you lead a better lifestyle?

Once you've identified your motivation, keep it right at the forefront of your mind. Never let it go.

TRICK YOURSELF

Having a goal isn't enough in itself to drive you on. There were always mornings when I felt that short-term temptation to stay in bed an hour longer rather than go for a run. Or I'd feel that drive to leave the gym early so I could see my kids before they went to bed.

Everyone, no matter how driven and committed they are, has these moments. It can be difficult to think of future benefits when your bed is warm. Your brain is a lazy fucker. It likes doing things that feel good. But it's not very clever at choosing between the different sorts of feeling good. As far as your brain is concerned, it's much less effort to get those nice feelings from playing a game on your phone than it is to get them from finishing the work you need to do for that day. It's quicker and it's easier, which is why you end up playing Angry Birds for eight hours straight rather than finishing that report. If you leave it up to your brain, it'll pick the Mars bar over the kale smoothie every day of the week.

But it's possible to trick your brain into weighing things up differently by emphasising to yourself both the pleasure you'll feel if you achieve your long-term goals and the misery you'll experience if you let them fall by the wayside.

41

One thing that really helped me to get out of bed on those cold winter mornings was to think about how amazing it would be to win a world championship. If I didn't get up, then I'd never get the chance to walk out at Goodison. I also thought about what would happen if I didn't persist. I'd think about how angry and bitter abandoning my dream of becoming world champion would leave me, and the impact that would have on Rachael and the children.

I knew that I'd only be cheating myself and I didn't want to let that become a habit. I'd seen what had happened to some of the other lads who I'd started out training alongside. They'd let go of their motivation. There was never a big moment when they said, 'Fuck this, I don't want to be a boxer any more.' It was more an accumulation of smaller incidents. They'd turn up later and later at the gym and then one day, you'd realise they hadn't turned up at all. The thought of that happening to me killed me. I knew that come the end of the day, I'd already be regretting not having got up. But more than that, I was already afraid of ending up washed-up and bitter, blaming everyone else when deep down, I knew that my failure was my fault and my fault alone.

THE PLEASURE OF PROVING OTHER PEOPLE WRONG

You're a bullshitter until the moment that you actually achieve something. For a very long time, a lot of people thought I was a bullshitter, which was fair enough. I was actually guilty of the odd white lie when I was a kid, mostly the result of overenthusiasm on my part: 'I know him, he's my cousin' (he wasn't). 'Yeah, I can sort that out for you' (I couldn't). Boxing was different, it meant more. Almost as soon as I'd formulated my ambition, I started telling people about it. Over and over again. I'd tell them that I was going to become world champion at Goodison Park. I'd tell them that I was going to be the best fighter who'd ever come from this city. I had absolutely no right to say any of this. I'd achieved the square root of fuck all.

I'm not one for all that see-believe-achieve shit. What I did realise, however, was that the more I ran my mouth off, the more pressure there'd be on my shoulders to prove that I wasn't actually a bullshitter. In the meantime, I had to live with the constant noise of people criticising me or laughing at me.

But that was the best motivation I could ever have. And that was the mentality I kept with me throughout my career. My whole time in boxing was about proving people wrong.

When people said I was full of shit or when they looked at me and told me to 'Be realistic, you've got no chance,' that would drive me even more. When later on I lost fights and people said, 'You're not going to be able to cut it in the pros,' I didn't stop. 'OK,' I'd tell them, 'we'll see. I'll get there.' Every knock that people gave me only pushed me on further. The more people told me I was chatting shit, the more I wanted to prove them wrong.

When I was a kid starting out, every Boxing Day I met up with my closest mates to have a good bevvy and a good laugh. I remember there was one year when one of my friends' dad's mates was ripping me.

'You're a good lad,' he said, 'but you're not going to make it, are you?'

He made sure all of my mates in the pub could hear him and I knew he wanted to embarrass me. That set me off.

'Listen, lad. I'm going to be rich,' I told him. 'I'm going to be so fucking rich you wouldn't understand. I'm going to own the company.'

I could see he wasn't buying that at all.

'Fuck off,' he said. 'Don't be stupid. You're just an amateur boxer. Don't be ridiculous.'

All I said in reply was, 'You'll see.'

I saw this fella again about four years ago and I said, 'That worked out all right, didn't it, lad?' And he just laughed. He tried to crack on he didn't know what I was on about. But he knew. He 100 per cent knew.

My desire to prove people like him wrong was one of the things that kept me going during the hard times. And gradually, painfully slowly, after years of me forcing this pipedream down so many people's throats, they, too, started to think I could make it happen.

I definitely don't think you should willingly open yourself to as much abuse as I got (and probably deserved), but going public with your plans can end up being really useful. If you announce the night before to anyone – it could be your girlfriend or a mate – that you're going to go to the gym or sign up for that half-marathon, then you'll be putting a subtle amount of pressure on your shoulders. Who wants to look foolish or weak for not keeping their promises? It's a good tool to have up your sleeve ahead of those days when you know you're going to be that bit more vulnerable to temptation. And it's another example of how to trick that lazy brain out of choosing the easiest option.

YOUR PERFORMANCE IS IMPORTANT – EVERYBODY ELSE'S IS IRRELEVANT

I had days when I looked around the Rotunda and caught sight of the ease with which one of the other lads ran, or the power and grace of a more naturally gifted fighter's left hook, and I'd think: *I'll never be able to do that.* If I wasn't careful, that thought could lead to other ones: *This isn't fair. They were born with so much more than me. What's the point?*

There were days when having that drive and desire to reach their level helped. It also taught me how dangerous it was to spend too much time comparing myself to other people and what they could do. I was determined never to let it become an excuse. Ultimately, the gifts that they were born with were completely irrelevant to me and my goal. The only thing that I could control, and the only thing that was important to me, was *my* progress. All I could do was try to ensure that I left the gym each day in a better position than I'd been in when I walked through its doors. If I could use the idea of keeping up with that guy who was absolutely smashing it in the gym as inspiration, then brilliant, but apart from that, his performance had nothing to do with me or my own progress. So why would I give it a second thought?

Don't judge yourself by other people's standards. It doesn't matter how well other people are doing, how much further than you they're running, how much more than you they're earning. All that counts is your own performance.

CHANGES

The destination might stay the same, but always be alive to the need to make changes to the route you're taking to get there. What might work for you one month won't necessarily be good the next month. Interrogate what you do and why. For a long while, the part-time jobs I worked were essential in subsidising my boxing, but a point came when they started to act as an impediment.

When you go to make changes, be wary of the temptation of making changes for change's sake. Make sure you're clear about what advantages you're getting out of that switch. You shouldn't see it as a Hail Mary pass to try when you can't think of anything else to do. Later in my career, I ended up changing trainers. I didn't do that just because I wanted to see a fresh face in the gym (although that does have its own value) or because I'd run out of ideas, but because I'd done the research and I knew the exact ways that the new coach could help me to improve.

SUMMARY

- Find what you're prepared to get punched in the face for. What's your purpose? You need something to fix your eyes on when times get tough.

- Write down your strengths and weaknesses. Be honest. It should feel a bit uncomfortable.

- Set realistic, achievable goals.

- Trick your brain by focusing on the benefits of what you want to do while weighing up the negatives of not achieving your targets. This is how brains work – yours isn't broken.

- Don't listen to the negative voices. In fact, use them as motivation.

- Focus on yourself, not other people. You can't control them. They don't matter.

CHAPTER 2
SECONDS IN

Brooks is a giant. He seems out of place in this tiny social club; like he'd be more comfortable scaring the shit out of villagers as he stomps their houses into matchsticks or rampaging from skyscraper to skyscraper in New York. He's so big that his kit is barely able to contain his body. His shorts, his head guard, even his boots are all bursting at the seams. When he moves across the canvas, I swear I can feel the room shake.

Midway into the first round, his big howitzer of a right hand catches me and the lights flash. I fall into the ropes and the referee starts his count. These are both new experiences for me, and I don't like either. I'm annoyed that I've been knocked down, but I'm outraged that the referee has intervened.

'What are you counting for?' I'm incandescent. So angry that I'm barely aware of anything except my own sense of injustice. Everything else – the bewildering pain Brooks has caused me, the raucous crowd, even Jimmy's bulky form in my corner – has faded.

The referee ignores me and carries on; he's up to five now.

By the time he gets to eight, I've had enough. 'You've just counted me to eight for no reason. Move out of the way.'

Second round I do him with a right-hander. Boom, kid's out. Game over.

I'm fucking high off myself after that. I get back to the corner and start into my familiar braggadocio: 'You've just witnessed the fucking bollocks out there. I am the business. I am better than anyone here.' My words spin out into the smoke-filled room. Everyone is staring at me like I'm a lunatic. Everyone except Jimmy, who gives me a slap on the face and drags me back to the dressing room.

'Why was the referee counting me?'

'Cos the fucking kid does you. He knocked you back into the ropes. You looked a bit dazed.'

'No I wasn't. Don't tell me I was dazed, you big fucking dope.'

'I'll tell you, because someone fucking needs to.'

There are some people who change your life. Jimmy Albertina was the greatest boxing coach I've ever worked with. He was also one of the best men I've ever known.

It was Micky Whitty, an amateur boxer who I knew from security work, who persuaded me to try the Rotunda ABC again. Mick was a good ten years older than me, a feared lad on the street and game as fuck. He told me I should give it a go. We were the same weight, so we could spar together: 'It'll be brilliant. We'll nail each other. We'll bring each other on so much. Albo is the best coach you'll ever meet.'

Yes, I thought to myself, *I'll have a bit of that.*

At Stockbridge ABC I'd been coached by Mark Kinney,

a great guy whom I felt like I was learning a lot from, but he'd just taken a job at Jaguar. He was on a different shift pattern, which meant that two out of three weeks he wouldn't be able to be in the gym. I didn't trust anybody else to coach me, so that was it.

That first day when I went back to the Rotunda it was with my tail between my legs. Almost two years had passed and yet Jimmy looked at me without surprise, like he'd been expecting to see me again.

'All right, lad, you're back.'

I swallowed my pride and asked if they'd let me train. He had a little dig at me and that was it. I was in.

The Rotunda used to be spit and sawdust, a shithole, stinking gym opposite the Easby Estate, which, like any area in Liverpool, had its fair share of lunatics. It was just one compact building. Nothing was new there, not the battered floor nor the ancient gym equipment that seemed as if it had been scavenged rather than bought. I fucking loved it. I loved the infamous gloves room with its rows of Mexico Reyes gloves and stench of decades-old sweat. It was boss. I even loved the matted area in the far left corner where we did the circuits that Jimmy was obsessed by and I hated with a passion.

Nobody cared that the gear was shitty or the area was rough, because the Rotunda ABC was like a factory turning out champions and at the centre of it all was Jimmy. He was small and thickset, a fat little hardcase who might have been a brilliant fighter if he hadn't liked a pint and good scoff so much. What was odd was that he wasn't at all flabby – every part of his body was like rock. His legs, thighs and calves were the biggest I've ever seen. He was like a Scouse Roberto Carlos. And you couldn't miss them, because he was always in cycling shorts. He'd just wobble round the gym in a vest, his big round belly sticking out in front of him, giving out a constant stream of advice. He was so funny, so down-to-earth, and his whole personality permeated right through that gym.

Without Jimmy Albertina, I wouldn't be the man I am today. I've had other great coaches. Terry Quinn taught me how to box. Mark Kinney was a fantastic guy. Noel Quarless helped a lot. All of these men played their part; they all helped me along the way, but it was Jimmy who was the most prevalent person in my life.

Everybody was devoted to him, even those kids who were so out of control even their own parents had given up on them, and they all respected him. They just loved him. In return, he loved us all, looked after us as if we were his own. He was definitely another father figure for me. You could have a laugh with him, but you'd never ever cross him. You'd never answer him back, because you had so much respect for him.

I started working with the likes of Mick Whitty and Paul Ghia. I got to meet Joseph Selkirk, who was a baby of thirteen at the time. I never looked back after that, not once. I just knew that gym was the making of me. It turned out that Jimmy had been watching my first steps in amateur boxing. He'd been there the night I knocked out Ryan Cunliffe when I had a fucked rib. He was there, telling everyone around him: 'Watch this kid, he's got ability.' Then, once I'd turned up at the Rotunda, Jimmy had called Mark Kinney, who'd told him two things. One, that one day I'd be a national champion. Two, that I hated fitness work. 'Anything he does that involves punching or hurting people,' Mark said, 'he does with a smile on his face. But he can't stand doing circuits and he can't stand running.'

Jimmy repeated this conversation to me. The excited glow that had begun to spread in me when he told me about Mark's faith that I could become a champion was quickly stopped when he explained that he'd be giving me twice as many circuits as any other fighter in the gym.

'I'm going to make you run,' he said, 'at the same speed I make the fucking featherweights run.'

'For fuck's sake, Jimmy.'

'You love sparring, you love punching pads and bags, and Mark was right, you love hurting people.'

'I know, yeah, that's what boxing's about.'

'No it's not. It's about being as fit as you can be and the punching will take care of itself. I know what you're good at, Anthony, but I also know what your weaknesses are.'

I'd never had a coach speak to me like that. He saw so clearly that I had to improve my stamina, my sharpness, my explosiveness, my punching power and my basic fitness. I hadn't understood the importance of any of that, but slowly, surely, I realised how right Jimmy was.

I arrived at the Rotunda knowing I was decent and think-ing I might have potential, but in truth, I hadn't the first idea what boxing was really about. I'd soon learn. At the Rotunda, they showed me how to train. It was so regimented there and it felt as if you were part of a proper team. When you went in, everyone was working their bollocks off, going right at it. There wasn't even one person slacking. They demanded the best from every single fighter. I remember standing there and feeling that all I wanted in the world was to be part of that. Over and over in my head I was saying: 'This is the place for me. This is the place for me.'

Rotunda ABC had turned out champion after champion – four or five of them every single year. Without fail. New kids, old kids. Most of the lads there had been fighting since they were nine – they were amazing athletes. Things like circuits were easy for them. When we went out for jogs, they all looked as if they could keep on running for ever. For the first time since I'd started boxing, I was really struggling to keep up. Nowadays, some of the people I trained with back then will say, 'I was in the gym with Tony Bellew.' In my head, they're still the stars – as far as I was concerned, I was in the gym with *them*.

The coaches – alongside Jimmy there was Mick McAl-lister, John Doolan, Michael McNally, George Whittaker, John Wignall and John Warburton – showed me the levels of sacrifice and dedication you needed to get to the top. They focused on strength, stamina and tactics, leaving no stone unturned. But the best thing they helped me with was making me use my feet more in boxing matches. I'd always been able to punch and I always wanted to meet my opponents head-on, but for the first time now I'd use my feet as well as fists as weapons. The coaches at the Rotunda taught me not only how to use my feet to get myself out of trouble, but also how to use them to dictate the range of fights.

That's something I'd keep with me throughout my career. In all the years I've boxed, sparring, pro, amateur, whatever, Oleksandr Usyk is the only fighter with better feet than me. Some of that was my natural talent, but a big chunk of it was owing to the lessons I learned in that funny little gym in the North End of Liverpool.

Jimmy would always be there, chirping away. All I wanted to do was impress him. I was desperate for his approval. My dad would tell me how brilliant I was after each victory. He told me I was going to be a world champion. But that wasn't enough, because of course my dad would say that. But I *needed* to hear those things from Jimmy. I *needed* to hear him say, 'Lad, that was fucking brilliant.' He never once did.

Jimmy wasn't soft. He wasn't a man who'd say nice things for the sake of saying them. And he understood that keeping us motivated wasn't just a question of telling us we were brilliant every second of the day. But Jimmy cared so deeply about us. That's why he could sometimes be harsh.

At the time of writing, I still hold the record for the quickest knockout in the country. It was a novice Under 10s final in 2003 at Knottingley Sports Centre in Leeds against a guy called Ahmed who was 10 and 0. It took six seconds – six seconds and he was stone cold. I hit him so hard on the chin that he fell flat on his face. I knew as soon as my glove slammed into his jaw that he wasn't going to get up.

I felt no pain, like you might expect. First, there was what felt like an electric bolt surging up my arm, right through to the shoulder. Then everything in his body just stopped. No movement, nothing. The referee didn't even bother counting. I walked over to his corner and climbed up onto his section of his ropes. I looked around the hall, made sure everybody was watching, then yelled: 'I'm the best fucking fighter youse lot will ever see.' The *cheek* of me. When I look back, I'm embarrassed.

I swaggered back to my corner, waiting for Jimmy to tell me how brilliant I was. He didn't miss a beat.

'Fucking shit that, lad.'

Then there was me boxing at Everton Park, after I'd been out injured for a spell. I stopped the kid in the first round. I blitzed him and I was shouting to all the people, all of his fans, 'I'm back, I'm fucking back. I've told you I'm back now. Look what I've done to him. I'm back.'

I got back to the corner, and Jimmy grabbed hold of my head guard and said, 'You're back?! Where have you fucking been, you stupid dickhead?'

But behind the scenes, when I was out of earshot, as he sat there chatting to his mates like John Doolan and Mick McAllister, he was saying something different: 'That kid's going to be special.' And what Jimmy actually did for me was far more important than anything he could possibly have said.

Jimmy knew that it didn't matter how good your footwork was or how hard you could punch – people didn't really pay attention until you were put on the right stage. And if he thought you had something about you, he'd put you forwards. Jimmy wasn't willing to waste his time. He only kept fighters at the Rotunda who he thought could cut it. Which is why from time to time a lad would disappear from view. Nobody would ask about them or saying anything; they'd just be gone. If you weren't good enough, you wouldn't get bouts, you wouldn't be entered into competitions. Eventually, you'd get the message. But Jimmy always wanted to work on me. He always wanted me to be out there fighting for Rotunda. That should have told me. It didn't matter how many times he called me a fucking idiot, it was Jimmy Albertina who put me on that stage to shine.

You lose people in life. Jimmy died from a heart attack in 2003. My uncle had passed away from cancer not long before that, but I could process that, because I'd had time to prepare for it. Jimmy going so suddenly felt like the hardest thing I'd ever had to take. I was still so young that I didn't understand the grief that seized me. He'd had a quadruple bypass in the spring of that year and it was fine for a while. I used to go and visit him. On a Friday after the gym, I'd go straight to his and hang out with him before I had to go and work on the doors.

He'd usually be watching television. *Taggart* was his favourite and he'd make a big thing of being annoyed.

'You've come round and disturbed my programme. Bernie, stick that on record, so I can talk to this lad while he's coming.'

Of course, he was delighted that I was there. Part because he liked my company and part because he could plug me for information about the gym he wasn't even supposed to be thinking about while he was recovering.

'Lad, what workout have you done tonight? Tell me exactly what workout you've done and what circuit you've done at the end.'

When I told him, he'd be enraged.

'That cheeky fucker, he's changed my workout. I'll fucking slap him.'

Oh my God! He cared so much, he couldn't ever stop caring.

Losing him was a catastrophe. I remember it was another Rotunda fighter, Paul Smith, who phoned me on a Monday morning.

'Jim is dead.'

'What are you talking about?' I said. 'I was only with him on Friday. What are you on about? You're not making any sense?'

He was crying dead loud down the phone. He said, 'Jimmy. He's dead.'

It felt as if the world was coming down. All I could think was, *oh no, what the fuck*. Selfish shit that I was, this was followed by another thought: *What the fuck am I going to do now for boxing? Is it over?*

We all went to the gym. What else could we have done? Jimmy had all sorts of fellas coming and going in the gym. I think he liked the noise and energy that came with it.

There was this one lad who was always on the rob – books, vitamins, tablets, DVDs . . . there wasn't a WHSmith in a ten-mile radius that was safe from him – and he'd brought Jimmy an Everlast tank top. I was going through this phase of thinking I was a rapper and basketball player, so this vest caught my eye immediately.

'Jimmy, give us that top. You're never going to wear that. It won't fit you. It'll look great on me.'

'No, lad, it'll look great on me with my cycling shorts. Leave it alone.'

I kept pestering him and pestering him. In the end, he said, 'Go on, lad, just take it. Just fuck off and get out my office.'

That day Jimmy died, I drove round to the Rotunda in my mum's car – I didn't even have a driving licence – and sat with Paul, crying in that top, feeling absolutely broken and devastated. It was the first time I'd ever felt grief. The whole gym was there. We were all stunned. It was horrible; it took a really long time to recover. A really, really long time.

The funeral was the biggest I'd ever seen. He'd trained maybe fifty amateur national champions. Any one of them would have carried his coffin when he died. But I was nominated as one of the six men who'd have that honour, which was a huge surprise to me: it was the first time I realised how much Jimmy had thought of me. There were two champions from the past, two from the present and two who he believed would have a brilliant future. I was in that final pair. At the time, all I had to my name was a novice title. Somehow, even after he'd passed away, Jimmy had found a way of making me feel as if I could conquer the world.

After that, the gym was shut for quite a bit. The next time I boxed, it was at the end of the year at the novice Amateur Boxing Association (ABA) championships. I dedicated the title to Jimmy. I cried after I won, because I knew that Jimmy should have been there watching me. Everything I've gone on to achieve in the years since has only been possible because of Jimmy and the impact he had on me. I'm still close with his children; his wife, Bernie, was at my wedding. I still have that Everlast vest. I still think of him every day.

Luckily, I had someone by my side to help me through my sadness. A couple of years before, I'd met a girl called Rachael Roberts. Or to be more accurate, I met her again. It was in the silly hours of the morning and I'd been working at the nightclub in the basement of Club 051. I'd started out there as a glass collector when I was fifteen. That lasted for about three weeks and then I strangled someone.

That night I had been going about my business quietly, when some fella pushed me out of the way. I ignored him and picked up another empty glass. For whatever reason, he carried on giving me hassle, so I got him by the neck and belted him a couple of times. He stopped pushing me after that; largely because it's difficult to push anybody when you're flat on your back.

They moved me to do the security on the DJ box after that. I was given a radio and the instruction that I wasn't to do anything stupid like throw anybody out. I just had to raise the alarm to the boys on the door if I spotted trouble anywhere in the club.

Footballers loved that place. You'd see Paul Ince bowl in and smoke twenty ciggies. They'd all want to get in that DJ box while everyone around them was getting off their cakes. I'd work on the Saturday then head to school the following Monday full of stories. 'You should have seen . . .' Everyone thought I was chatting shit, because I told them all the crazy things I'd seen.

On that particular night, I'd finished working my security shift at the DJ box and was on my way up to do an after-hours club called Sunrise, when a girl stopped me just as I was about to walk in. She was absolutely beautiful. Gorgeous body. Lovely face. Dark hair, dark eyes. Everything you could possibly want.

And then she called me Anthony, which caught me off guard. I thought, *no one calls me Anthony in this area that I know; it's either Bellew or Bomber, or Little Ant.*

'Anthony, Anthony,' she persisted.

I looked and then said, 'All right,' which isn't one of

61

the all-time great opening lines, but in my defence, it was 4 a.m.

She went, 'It's Rachael.'

All I could say was, 'I don't know a Rachael that looks like that.'

'It's Rachael Roberts, Neil's sister.'

Fucking hell. Wow, she's grown up, I thought. *She didn't look like that the last time I saw her.*

I'd actually known her since I was eleven and she was ten, when I used to knock around with her brothers, Neil and Ashley. Then they moved house, time flashed on and I didn't see her for years.

I remember saying to her, 'Are you going in?'

I took her and her mate, Rhian, to the front of the queue, got them in for free and then couldn't stop thinking about her. And now here we are, twenty years later.

I'd never trusted women before. I think working in nightclubs – seeing girls sniffing all kinds of drugs, going with all kinds of men, doing absurd things in the toilets – made that hard. But I trusted Rachael from the very first second. I'd known her since she was a kid. I knew her family were good people. I've never really felt as if I've deserved her and I've not always been a perfect husband, but I adored her then and I adore her now. She keeps me in line: when I'm being an idiot, she won't speak to me; she doesn't even want to know me.

More than that, she's been a driving force in my life. I've always wanted to prove to her that I'm worth all the hassle.

Being with her helped to sharpen my ambitions. I realised that by fighting, I could get her everything she'd wanted but couldn't have as a kid. If I hadn't had her by my side over the years, then I know I'd have veered off down the wrong path. It's her and our kids who have kept me on the straight and narrow. Without them, I'd be nowhere.

SURROUND YOURSELF WITH GOOD PEOPLE

While it's true that the ultimate responsibility for your fate always has to rest on your shoulders, you'll inevitably end up relying on other people at some stage on your journey. Everyone needs a helping hand from time to time. That's why the human beings you surround yourself with are so important. You need to establish as early as you can who genuinely wants the best for you and who's only interested in themselves.

In my time in boxing, I've been lucky to see human beings at their best. The Rotunda was full of people who were desperate for me to become the finest possible version of myself I could be. I was shaped by that scrappy room and the hard, brave, funny men who trained us. Their expertise made me work so much harder than I would have anywhere else. They encouraged me, but they were also unafraid to give me hard lessons when they felt I needed them. The Rotunda coaches are the reason I became an ABA champion and a regular international boxer.

But I've also seen people at their worst and I'm still scarred by some of my experiences. I've learned that you should never be friends with people who are jealous of your success, or who want something from you, or who lie or talk shit about you behind your back. If you feel worse every time you see somebody, you should stop seeing them as soon as you can.

All that is why I believe that when you find good people – whether it's in your personal or professional life – you should do the hard work of treating them well and keeping them close.

WATCH OUT FOR SHARKS

I wish everybody was good. I wish everybody was more like Jimmy Albertina. But they're not and it's dangerous to pretend otherwise. I went into boxing with that belief and before long, I got done over. That's why I have always kept a very tight circle around me. I've seen too many fighters have the life sucked out of them by the leeches that hang on to them right up until the moment they realise that there's no money left.

Very few people are interested in helping you. There was never a moment when an older fighter turned to me and said, 'Here's the secret. This is what you need to know about the boxing world.' Nobody helps anybody else. There were a couple of occasions when I was younger, before

I'd learned this hard lesson, when I reached out to other fighters. Instead of helping me, they tried to sabotage my career. It was so blatant, as if they weren't even bothered about me finding out.

One time, a little after I'd decided to turn professional, I approached another boxer, who used to be a good friend, and asked him to put in a good word for me with Frank Warren. *No problem*, he told me. I'd done him favours in the past and it seemed like the least he could do. Warren never called, which was odd given that by that time I was a three-time ABA champion, the best prospect in this country; two of those final victories were by knockouts. In one of them, I rendered the other guy unconscious for five minutes – something that hasn't been done before or since – live on television with all the promoters watching.

A year passed. A couple of other promoters approached me to turn pro with them, but the money wasn't right and because Rachael and I had already had Corey by then, I decided to stay as an amateur. Then one day in 2007, I sparred with a guy called John Anthony, a powerful, unbeaten cruiserweight at Dave Coldwell's gym. I was butchering him, smashing him all over the gym. I punched holes in him. Dave turned to me. 'Why don't you go pro?' he asked. I explained what had happened with my friend.

Dave was bewildered by what I told him. Right there and then, in front of me, he called Frank.

'I've found a TV fighter for you.'

I could hear Frank's voice coming faintly over the line.

'What do you mean?'

'I've got this kid in my gym and I've just watched him take my fighter apart. He didn't even break into a sweat.'

'What's his name?'

'Tony Bellew.'

'I've heard of him. I know who he is. Ask him to come to my office on Monday.'

So my dad and I drove up to London. I walked in past the bronze Prince Naseem statue in the hallway, still in a state of shock. It was Frank Warren, a man who created champions like other guys made breakfast. *This was it*, I thought. I told Frank about my previous attempt to contact him. All he told me was that he trusted Dave's judgement.

'If he says you're a TV fighter, then you're a TV fighter.'

He asked me what I'd been offered before. I told him and he promptly doubled it, sweetened by a ten-grand signing-on fee. I was skint, I had a kid and a mortgage and nowhere to go, and it was fucking unbelievable money. There was nothing to think about. All I asked him was how many times a year I could fight: 'As many times as you want.'

A couple of years later, I asked Dean Powell, Frank's right-hand man, why they hadn't signed me first time round.

'We were told you were too fat and lazy to make light heavyweight.'

I'd been done over by that man I'd thought was a friend, who came from the same city as me, who trained in the same amateur gym as me. I should have known – I'd seen him do the same to others.

I don't regret what happened and I don't hold it against him. He was just looking out for himself. If he could keep me out of the limelight, his own chances of making it would have been improved. Maybe not by much. Anyway, I wish him well and hope he's doing OK. It's sad – he was a good fighter.

It was a lesson: never mix friendship and pound notes, ever. Just. Don't. Do. It. As far as I'm concerned, business is business. I've become very cold-hearted like that. It meant that when Riddick Bowe once asked if he could join my training team, I gracefully had to tell him that I was happy with my team. He was the guy I'd grown up idolising – I couldn't risk my judgement being clouded.

I was even more hurt by Frank Warren when it all ended in the way it did. I was fiercely loyal to Frank Warren right until the end. I trusted him – that's why it hurt so much. We were friends, or at least I thought we were. He'd take me up to watch the Arsenal in his box at the Emirates. We talked for hours and hours about boxing. We'd text message each other all the time. So, when everything went wrong between us, it broke my fucking heart. I don't want to go over old ground here and I'm sure he'd tell a different story to me. But what it taught me is that I have to feel like I can trust and rely on everyone in my team completely. If that trust goes, you have to make the change. And for me, that change was Eddie Hearn.

THE IMPORTANCE OF TRUST

I've never had a contract with Eddie. There's not a single piece of paper that ties us together. But we've had a brilliant relationship because we both trusted each other. When he took me on, he might not have been the best promoter in the world – he certainly didn't have the power he does now – but I could tell he was the most honest. By the same token, I was just a scrappy, promising up-and-comer; he knew I was a risk. He took a chance on me and I've never forgotten that faith. So even later on, when I'd become a box-office star, one of the biggest draws in the country, and was getting solid offers of big money, I told him the same thing: 'I'm going to finish my career with you.'

There were times when I wanted to kill him because he'd thrown me into fights where I was getting tuppence. And there were times when I was phoned by other promoters offering to double my money if I binned off the bout Eddie had arranged for me and fought on their bill instead. I could have fucked Eddie over and taken that cash. But I didn't, because being loyal was important to me.

He stood by me, I stood by him and we stayed loyal to each other. I like to think that that means something. The strength of our relationship has helped to make us money, which is great. But more important than that was the knowledge that whatever happened, I could trust Eddie. When you trust someone, it means that when they tell you they're going to do something, you can be confident that they will. It means that you don't lie awake at night worrying that they might do you over. It means that you know that they'll always have your back.

I want to be able to trust people. And that's why I'll give you the benefit of the doubt. If I get second-hand information that you've been having a bit of a jangle about me, I'm likely to say, 'Oh well, you never know.' It's only when you've nailed me and it can't be anything but that that I just go, *fuck you*. And that's it – you're gone. I'll remove you from my life. You'll never get another chance. No matter how close you are, no matter what we've been through. I won't, can't, ever trust you, and that's it. Someone who's done you over once will probably do it again.

If you can't trust somebody, then you shouldn't keep them around you. If you do, there will always be that shadow lurking in the background. You'll spend your life wondering whether they're lying to you or plotting behind your back. And then at some point down the line – it might be sooner, it might be later, but it will come – they'll turn round and fuck you.

DO UNTO OTHERS AS YOU WOULD HAVE DONE UNTO YOU

I've always lived by the motto: treat others how you would expect to be treated yourself. I've never done wrong by anybody who didn't have it coming to them.

If you've got good people around you, make sure that they feel trusted and valued. If you're the kind of boss who treats your best employees like shit and constantly ignores their requests for a raise, don't be surprised if they walk out of the door. If you're the sort of friend who walks on by when your mates need you, then you can't expect them to have your back when you're in trouble.

Don't treat relationships like they're transactions. If you enter a friendship thinking to yourself: *What's in it for me?*, I guarantee it won't last. I've seen what boxing looks like when it's every man for themselves, and it's not pretty. That's why I help up-and-coming boxers – I want to give them the sort of nudge in the right direction I wish someone had offered me when I was in their position. I don't get any money from it, but I do get a buzz out of helping them. When you're lucky, pass it back down. You'll feel much better for it.

GOOD PEOPLE WILL CHALLENGE YOU

My mates Franny and Gary have been with me since the beginning. They've seen the highs and lows, ups and downs. Gary especially has been a constant presence at my side. He's maybe the person I'm closest to in and around my training camps. During the first phase of my professional career, I was training with Anthony Farnell up in Manchester. I was Commonwealth champion, knocking down every

70

opponent they put me up against, and in my head I was the best prospect in the world.

I liked the situation I had then. I was my own boss there and when I turned up, I was treated like a superstar. I'd bring my friends to watch me train every other day. We'd work out together – they'd tell me how fit I was and I enjoyed helping them to improve. But I wasn't being challenged by anybody. I was the only one who wanted to push themselves – everyone else seemed to be there for a good time. I didn't see that as a problem, but Franny and Gary both thought my focus was slipping.

Eventually, they took me to one side and told me: 'This place is no good for you. You're taking your friends to the gym. It's not a proper job. You're a really good fighter, but you should move gyms. Go back to Liverpool. If you don't make the right decisions, you're going to lose it all for yourself.'

What was clear to them wasn't clear to me. 'No,' I told them, 'I'm going to stay with Farnell. I'm all right. I like going there.'

It was only when we started preparations for my next bout that I had that sick feeling in the pit of my stomach: they were right, I was wrong. The environment in Manchester wasn't professional enough. It was too late by that point – I couldn't change in the midst of the training camp. But I knew it was over.

I got dropped twice in that fight. Not long afterwards, I changed coach and started training in Liverpool, just as Fran and Gary had suggested.

There's a difference between being the sort of person who blows smoke up their mates' arses and somebody who genuinely wants their friends to be the absolute best version of themselves they can be. Your real friends will have difficult conversations with you; they'll tell you when you're out of order. You won't always like what they're telling you, but make sure you listen, because sometimes they'll be right.

IT'S NOT ALWAYS ENOUGH TO BE NICE

Saying no is hard. When I was a fighter, I always said yes, to almost everything. That's changed as I've got older and realised you can't please everyone, because somebody who lives their life doing that ends up as a clown. If you don't ever say no, no matter how hard it might seem, nobody will ever take you seriously.

I'm soft, I care about people. My missus says it all the time. She reckons that if I got any more laid-back, I'd be asleep. And my kindness gets taken for weakness sometimes. That's happened throughout my life. The problem is, when your kindness gets taken for weakness, people take advantage of you and then you end up doing nasty things to them.

One way of avoiding those situations is to make sure you're consistent in your behaviour. If you set clear boundaries, it makes life more straightforward for you and for everyone around you. It enhances co-operation, and it saves time and hurt feelings. The people I work with know how I'll respond to a given situation. They know what I expect from them and what I expect from myself. For instance, I'm good at making it clear that there's a point beyond which somebody *cannot* push me, partly because I know that when I do overstep the mark, there's no going back.

I'm not suggesting that you should produce a formal list of rules whenever you start a new job or enter a new relationship, but try to do what you can to avoid falling into the grey zones that are so often the places where disagreement and bad feeling grow.

HARD CONVERSATIONS

You have to be straight with people. You can't duck awkward conversations. I know some fighters who just send their coach a text message saying: 'I'm going to move on. Thank you very much, that's it.' I've always believed in taking the time to sit down with them, no matter how nasty it'll be.

That's not to say I find these sorts of encounters easy. Especially when it's with somebody who means a lot to me. When you work closely with somebody – all those hours in the gym – you do end up caring for them, too. And sometimes I think I'm more aware of others' feelings than my own. I'm very anxious about offending people or making them feel bad about themselves. Twice in my career I've had to sack a coach. And each time I spent the drive on the way to meet them worrying the fuck out of myself. I then had to psyche myself up in my car before I went in to see them. As I sat there in the driver's seat, I told myself that what I was doing was the right thing for me, even if it wasn't going to be that good for them.

In one case, it was just because he wasn't experienced enough at that point in time. But I wasn't experienced enough, either, and at that stage in my career, I needed someone who'd been around a bit more. Almost all coaches I've worked with, perhaps with the exception of Dave Coldwell, are incredibly insecure and insensitive – it seems to go with the territory – so that was something I had to bear in mind. But at the same time, I had to prioritise my own needs over their feelings.

I've definitely had that horrible feeling before of going into a tough conversation really sure of what I wanted to say. But then as soon as I started speaking, I'd look at the other guy's face, see them getting upset or angry and then lose my nerve. To try to avoid this, on these occasions I spent time beforehand thinking about how the coach would feel and what emotions I might feel. I also reminded myself of how bad things would get if I didn't have that conversation, so that I could keep control and avoid getting swayed by sentiment.

My last bit of preparation was to work out what I'd say in advance. I decided that I'd give them a choice: we can either bring somebody else in to give a little help or we can go our separate ways, no hard feelings.

None of this preparation was enough to make the conversations easy or pleasant. But it was so much better that I'd found a way of getting my head in the right space. It also made the exchange more constructive than if I'd just gone in and told them they were shit and didn't want to work with them any more.

Ultimately, you should never forget that you're not responsible for the emotional well-being of others. Be thoughtful, be considerate, treat people respectfully, but remember that if you're not looking out for your own interests, nobody else will. If you do something for the right reasons, in the right way, then you shouldn't have any reason to feel bad.

SUMMARY

- Surround yourself with people who want to help you become the best version of yourself.

- Treating you well sometimes means telling you things you might not want to hear.

- If someone shows you who they are, believe them.

- Treat people well. It's the right thing to do and it also feels good.

- But never forget that saying no is OK. Treating other people well doesn't mean ignoring yourself.

- Have difficult conversations – your brain won't want to, but trick it to focus on the longer-term benefits and the damage it would cause if you try to duck every confrontation.

CHAPTER 3
FAIL TO PREPARE, PREPARE TO FAIL

I know I'm going to beat him. It's too fucking easy. I'm not stupid – I know there's a reason why David Dolan is a super-heavyweight Commonwealth gold medallist. I know he's won the ABAs. I know he's contested close to 100 fights and boxed for England for over six years whereas I've had fewer than 20 bouts. But I'm absolutely flying at the moment. When I sparred with him last month in Crystal Palace, I rocked him all over the place. The way I see it, I'm stronger, faster and more skilful than him. In my head, I'm just thinking: I'm better than you in every department. I wobbled you with sixteen-ounce gloves. When I hit you with ten-ounce gloves, I'm going to knock you clean out. It's not even going to be hard.

We touch gloves. Anticipation surges through me. I know I'm seconds away from being able to lose myself in the exhilarating mix of savagery and control only boxing brings me. I'm already looking forward to the moment when I'll catch him hard for the first time.

The bell goes and I'm excited by how strong I feel. There's a

*thrill that comes with being this powerful, this quick. Already I'm
beginning to imagine the rush I'll get when the referee counts him
out. Most wins have come easily to me so far in my career. I don't
see any reason why this will be any different.*

*My body is ready. But I soon discover that my mind is way off.
The first round is tight. And then he starts pulling away. After two
rounds he's three points ahead. After three his lead is up to five. The
fact that I'd knocked the fuck out of him while we were sparring
begins to look embarrassingly irrelevant. So what if I'm punching
like a professional? This is an amateur bout and his tip-tap style is
perfect for it. For every big bump I land on him, he taps me four
times. By the end there's a seven-point gap. It's hard to process what's
happened. Just minutes ago I was acting as if I'd already won. But
I've lost. I've lost badly. And I can't help thinking that I've brought
this on myself.*

Sometimes life feels like a hard, vicious struggle. And then,
occasionally, you have those spells where everything comes
together so perfectly that you almost can't believe the good
times will ever come to an end. The loss of Jimmy had
knocked me for six, but otherwise I felt like I was flying at
the Rotunda.

There was a reason why it was the best gym in the country. It had Joseph Selkirk, Mick Whitty, the Smith brothers,
Declan O'Rourke, Joseph McNally, Andy Holligan, kids who'd
won gold medals at youth tournaments all over the world.
There were twelve to fifteen international boxers in an
amateur outfit in Liverpool. That's insane.

I'd walk into that hall full of national champions, a shitty-arse kid from Wavertree, take my headphones off, put my boxing gear on, head straight to the stereo and put my CD on. That's how the other boxers knew that Bomber had arrived. I was different to the rest of them. Not better, but different. For one thing, I was the only South-ender there, everyone else was from the north of Liverpool. On that side of the city, they listened to dance music; that was their culture. I wore gold chains and wanted to listen to rap. Their reaction was always, 'What the fuck's he doing?' And yet nobody ever tried to stop me.

I look back now and I think, *you cheeky bastard*. But that's just the way I was. I wonder if it was a way of laying down a marker – challenging anyone else to make anything of the fact that I was an outsider there.

I'd been a tall, lanky developer when I'd first arrived at the Rotunda, but I was filling out now, growing into my body. I'd also acquired a deep understanding of both my abilities and my limitations. I knew I was never going to be one of those amazing dexterous fighters. That didn't suit either my physique or the portion of talent I'd been blessed with. So I didn't try.

On the other hand, I had crazy power in my punch, my footwork was really good and I could take a lot of punishment. And I had a brilliant boxing IQ. I was able to watch other fighters and very quickly evolve a plan to beat them. Then, once I was in the ring, I could think on my feet, which meant I could adapt my approach according to what the situation demanded. If I needed to pressure a fight, I could; if I needed to go onto the back foot and box, I could; if I needed to fight and make him miss, I could do that. I could fight southpaw; I could punch with either hand. I was never great at any of them, but I was good at all of them. Taken as a package, I knew I was a threat.

This was all allied to a ferocious desire and a deep resilience, and the fact that I was already trying to act and fight like a professional. Once you're being paid to box, there's not so much emphasis on technical ability; a skilful fighter can be overwhelmed by a less talented but hungrier opponent. That suited me down to the ground.

The other boxers all wanted to win matches on points. In all the years I fought as an amateur boxer I barely ever came across an opponent who could punch. There was maybe one, a six foot eight, seventeen-stone bruiser called David Price, where he'd touch me and I'd think, *fuck, I don't want to get hit by him again.* I didn't look so much at the technical aspect: I wanted to hurt people. Skill isn't enough in the professional business. When you're fighting four two-minute rounds then you can get by on pure technical ability. You cannot skill your way through the thirty-six minutes of a pro bout. At some stage you'll have to stand up and say: *Right, I've got to have it here; I've really got to get stuck in.*

I'd be like that all the time, even when I was sparring with my teammates in the gym. I'd dive in, chinning other fighters when we sparred. I was knocking the fuck out of professionals. I knew none of the lads I was fighting was my final destination. I just saw everyone as another obstacle I needed to trample over on my way to achieving my dream. It didn't matter who I was facing or what the stakes were, I'd have chewed my arm off to win. I was still telling anybody who'd listen that I was going to become world champion at Goodison Park. And I was still being called a liar and a maniac and a fucking idiot.

I wasn't bothered. I liked the way that my ambition and the way I carried myself set me apart from all of the other boxers. I was the only one who'd turn up to those tournaments and say 'I'm going to knock him out.' The other ones might have talked about winning, they might even have been very confident of victory, but none of them were boasting about the damage they were going to cause. Nobody else was going round shouting, 'I'm going to chin him – he's got no chance.' I might not have been the most talented amateur boxer out there, yet my approach made me a better prospect for the professional game than anybody I faced.

I had some of my greatest times as an amateur boxer, but it was really just a hurdle I had to leap over. Everything had gone so quickly for me. I had that first bout, won it, then made sure I had another one to check if it was a fluke. I won that. Then I started thinking about entering championships, just to see how I'd get on. I won them, so then I stepped up to the next rank, where I knocked out everyone I faced. Then

I went up to the next level. I wanted to find out how good I really was. Down they all went.

That's when my coaches told me to go to the full senior ABAs. Every single fighter there had fought fifty, maybe sixty amateur bouts. I'd only fought in eleven, and I was fighting at a level ten kilos above the two national titles I'd already won. My coach's line was: *you're just going in for a bit of experience.* My line was: *fuck that, I'm here to win. I'll fuck everyone and you're going to watch.*

No matter how well I was doing, I still had to go out there and work, because I needed money to subsidise my boxing. In those first years after I'd been expelled from school, I had job after job. First working as a lifeguard, then onto the railways, working the doors and a spell doing daytime security and finally in a pillow factory. My mate Chris Walker, who's now a brilliant journalist, got me that job. It was ideal because it was 7 a.m. until 4 p.m. and I had to be at the gym by five, which ruled out a normal nine-to-five.

But stuffing pillows was also hard graft – far harder than you'd think – and long hours. The only things that made it bearable were knowing that the money I was earning was helping me edge closer to my dream and the fact that I could listen to music while I worked.

By 2004, I was living with Rachael at my mum's and my life had started to follow a regular routine: work, bus, boxing. Every night after I'd finished my shift I'd get the 86 bus up to Smithdown Road, then the 27 from Lodge Lane in Toxteth, all the way through Anfield and finally Scottie Road, Kirkdale. You'd meet every kind of reprobate and scumbag you could possibly imagine on these buses. But I'd just keep my headphones on, turning up the music so loud that you couldn't hear anyone else speaking.

Sometimes, if I had the energy, I'd walk from work to the Rotunda. And that was the problem. As the ABAs approached, I noticed that more and more often I'd be fatigued by the end of the day. Duke and Mick McAllister had spotted this, too and asked me what was up.

I said, 'Nothing's up. I came here from work.'

That was fine for the build-up, but they were clear that this couldn't continue once the tournament actually started.

'You're going to have to give up one or the other.'

'What do you mean?'

Duke said, 'You're tired. You're working from seven in the morning until four in the afternoon. Then you come straight here and train like an absolute maniac. And then you're just repeating the same thing Monday to Friday, every day. It can't go on, not if you're serious about this.'

I asked my boss at the pillow factory if I could have a month off, unpaid. For the first two thirds of my training camp for the ABAs I carried on working there, but in the last month I stopped. And that was it. The only work I was doing was the odd weekend on the doors. For the first time, I really felt as if I was a full-time boxer. My initial thought was: *this is sound.* And yet, it was soon followed by another: *I've got to succeed now at this boxing.*

83

If I won the ABAs, I knew that I'd be able to get one of the scholarships Liverpool City Council were offering to elite athletes, which would put enough money in my pocket to allow me to keep going without having to go back to the pillow factory. A victory would also put me on the radars of all the top promoters, who I knew watched the finals when they were broadcast on television. If I lost, I'd have to think about going down another route. I'd passed the physical to join the fire brigade, so that was an option, but, really, my heart was with boxing. Nothing else had the same pull.

It was yet another reason to push hard. I remember saying to Rachael: 'I know I've done a few fucked-up things, but I've got a plan. I'm going to win the ABAs. I'm going to get National Lottery funding. I'm going to be on the GB squad. I'm going to be the best fighter in this country.' I could tell that this sounded stupid to her. I'd been acting like a typical young lad. Too many late nights, too much nonsense, too much trouble.

Her only response was to say, 'Great, but what's that got to do with me?'

'I need you by my side. I promise you, I'm going to stop fucking about and stop doing the silly shit I'm doing, and everything will work out all right.'

Whether or not she still thought I was talking shit – which she had every right to – she made that choice and stuck by me. It was up to me to do everything I said I would.

I had the hardest fight of my life up to that point on a Friday night at the Everton Park Sports Centre against a lad called Sam Sexton in the ABA quarter-finals. I'd got through the earlier rounds without much difficulty and then been drawn against Sexton, who was a really good fighter. He'd won multiple titles, fought regularly for England, had five times as many fights under his belt as I did and was generally considered to be the overwhelming favourite. Everyone thought I was going to get beaten. Except me, because I was a cocky fucker and wasn't much interested in anybody else's opinion.

The first two or three rounds were an endorsement of the conventional wisdom. Sexton was so tough, so heavy and so good at what he did – far better than anybody else I'd faced in my previous twelve fights. At the end of the first round I was down by one point. I was two down after the second round and by the last round I was five points adrift. I don't know why, but I just couldn't get started. I started asking myself: *Am I good enough? Do I belong at this level?*

When I went back to my corner, my coach, John Warburton, whose nickname was Sore Arse (I've no idea how he got it and was always too afraid to ask), gave me a slap.

'You go out there and you fucking show everybody in here what you're made of.'

It might have been the slap, or it might have been Warburton's short but forceful speech, or it might have been the horrendous fear of losing in front of my friends and my dad. I don't know. But whatever it was clearly had an effect on me. I came out and smashed him all over the place. I wobbled him, landing blow after blow before I caught him so hard with my right hand that I knocked him out on his feet.

The referee started counting him out and just as he reached eight, Sexton seemed to wake up. He grabbed the head guard's strap at the chin and ripped it off. That bought him five minutes to recover, which absolutely enraged me.

'You can't do that,' I protested. Then I started pleading with the referee: 'Let me at him.'

Sexton, who knew exactly what he was doing, just smiled. However, it didn't do him much good in the long run. Having started the last round five behind Sexton, I ended up five points ahead of him.

It felt like such a massive achievement in my fourteenth fight, not only to have beaten someone with Sexton's pedigree, but also to do it over four two-minute rounds. I realised that you don't really learn that much about yourself when you're coasting through fights; you do when you're made to suffer.

And I had suffered. It was the first time I'd had my nose cracked. I'd also smashed my hand, which wasn't ideal with my next fight two weeks away. Even three hours after the fight I had a slow stream of blood coming out of my nose. My hands were shaking and whenever I tried to eat anything, I puked it up almost straight away.

Like a maniac, I turned up to work on the doors later that night with swollen, still quivering hands and a trickle of blood running constantly down my face that I couldn't staunch, whatever I tried. All the other boys on the door looked at me with horror. That was the first time ever that my dad told me to go home. Proud as he was, he was also worried by the sight of his son's black-and-blue features.

For a minute or two, I tried to make my case – I wanted the £100 I'd get paid – but, ultimately, Dad won that argument: 'I own the firm. You'll get paid. Just go home, son, please.' He was backed up by Joey Lynch, who worked with him. Joey's brother, John, had won the ABAs a good few years ago and he always took an interest in me. He knew I was a good kid with a good future, which is why he'd sometimes pay me for staying at home rather than coming in to work. Joey was one of those guys who wanted to give kids every chance of making the best of themselves.

After all that, the rest of the competition felt pretty straightforward. In just my sixteenth amateur bout, I won the heavyweight ABAs, my first televised fight, shown on the BBC. I went in there against the reigning champion, a Royal Marine called Mick O'Connell. Almost everyone had written me off because it was my first year in the competition. Instead, I went in there and absolutely boxed his head off. I schooled him from start to finish, made him look like a novice; I flicked and rocked him and won 12–3. In the process proving *Boxing News*, who'd predicted an O'Connell victory, very wrong. Ha ha.

All of a sudden, I became aware of what I'd achieved. I'd made history in my gym by becoming their first ever heavyweight ABA champion. My family were so proud of me, too. In their eyes I was a superstar, because I'd been on the telly and in the paper. It was exhilarating, addictive. And after that I carried on improving at a drastic pace. The next time I faced Mick O'Connell, I knocked him cold in the second round. I didn't think anybody could stop me.

Then I got jolted. Something that I really needed. David Dolan and his tippy-tappy style had beaten me. Up to that point, I'd been so accustomed to thinking of myself as an inferior boxer that I'd work like a maniac to bridge the difference whenever I came up against someone new. This time, however, I hadn't spent any time thinking about the strengths that had won Dolan that gold medal or about how much more experienced he was than me. I was too busy congratulating myself on how good I'd been when we'd sparred. Normally I'd focus insanely hard before a fight, but this time I was just looking forward to chinning him. Which, of course, was a massive mistake.

I'd got so accustomed just to turning up and smoking my opponents that I'd forgotten that there's no progression, no success, without struggle. I'd forgotten that if I wanted to get to the next level, I'd have to go through some hard times.

I started to shift my priorities. It wasn't enough to fight like a professional in the ring – I had to act like one outside it. Up until then, I might have worked hard in the gym, but I'd always been up for going out on the ale with my mates at the drop of a hat. If I got the call, ten minutes later I'd be there. Now, I'd go three or four months without touching a drop. If I did go out, the timing would be planned with military detail to make sure it never interfered with my training. That fucked off Rachael no end – the sacrifices I was starting to make to help further my ambitions inevitably had an impact on her life. But that became extra motivation: I had to make this work, because I didn't want to put her through that hardship and then have nothing to show for it.

The way to make it work was to give boxing every single ounce of energy I had in my body. I knew that from this point on, I couldn't afford to skip a beat. I couldn't afford to miss a session, I couldn't afford to have a week off here or there. Maybe I was better than any other fighter at this level, but there were so many steps I had to take, so many hurdles I had to leap over. The guys I'd have to beat to achieve my dreams were already way ahead of me.

I swore that whatever happened in my career, however far I got, I'd never let myself get undone by complacency, laziness or a lack of preparation. If I got beaten by a better boxer, fine, I could live with that. If I lost to a bad call by a referee, that would hurt but I'd cope. But if I got a hiding because I was unfit or hadn't got my head right, I knew that I wouldn't be able to forgive myself. Ever.

That attitude drove me on and on, through the last stretch of my amateur career and into the early stages of my time as a pro. Every time I went up a level, I worked even harder. What had started as a hobby was now an obsession.

*

Even if I was knuckling down, there were lads around me who had different ideas. There's a point early in your career when you're fighting nobodies, when you could, if you wanted to, piss around and still win. I know plenty of men who did. There's one thing that they have in common: they all failed. Frankie Gavin is Britain's only ever amateur world champion. He was training alongside me in Manchester when we'd turned professional. He could have been anything he wanted to be. He had so much more ability than me, it was actually stupid. All he needed to do was take things seriously.

While I was fighting for six grand every blue moon, when he first turned pro he was getting £50,000 for four-round fights. That is *obscene*. That is unheard of. He contested maybe ten bouts, made half a million quid and in all that time didn't face anyone with a winning record. He had an amazing talent but could never take life seriously, so his career just faded.

And then there was Joseph Selkirk. I'd known Joseph for a long time. I'd trained alongside him for the ABAs and he was without doubt the best fighter I've ever seen. That's not hyperbole – he was a simply unbelievable boxer. He had a street fighter's aggression allied to insane levels of skill. His boxing brain was off the chart. Joseph had everything. He trained hard when he was in the gym, but I swear to God, he didn't need to. This fella could have three weeks off, then turn up at the gym, get put in a sparring session and absolutely play with someone.

What he didn't have was the same mentality as I did. He didn't have the same drive. Some days he'd be raring to go, others he couldn't have appeared any less interested. While we were still amateurs and training as a team, you didn't notice it so much. It was only when we turned pro, and suddenly there was a lot more individual responsibility, that it showed.

Joseph was a really nice kid. I loved him. I always have and I always will. In fact, he's like a little brother to me. I'd always tried to look out for him because I didn't feel like he had anyone; he lost his dad in tragic circumstances when he was young. Our bond endured even when someone tried to come between us by telling lies. And because I couldn't bear the idea of him wasting his talent, I took him to training with me when I turned professional. Every day for a whole year, I'd drive the six miles to his house, pick him up, then take him to Manchester.

Some days I'd be waiting outside his house for him to get out of bed. On other days I'd be screaming at him. Occasionally he'd be great, but too often I'd get there and he'd just say, 'I can't be bothered today.' When, later on, I left Manchester and came back to the Rotunda, I brought him with me. For a while he was back on it: the training and coaches were so much better in Liverpool. And yet, gradually, I could see that he just didn't want to do it. There was no money in it for him at that point and I don't think he had the love for the game that I did.

Everyone wants to be rich. Everyone wants to be top of

the bill. But for him, the end goal was just too distant. He wasn't willing to put up with the struggle that's needed to get there. He wanted the nice stuff right there and then.

I care about him and still speak to him now; he was at my wedding, he was at my kids' christenings and he's someone who will always be part of my life. But it kills me that he didn't get where his talent demanded he should have. He had ten times the ability I had. If you'd have been able to stick my mindset on him, he'd have become the greatest fighter this country has ever produced. It's probably too late in the day now – he's into his thirties – and yet, I know he could still come back now and piss the British title, probably the European title, too. If I got him the right world title fight, I'm guessing he'd probably fuck them, as well.

What I knew and Joseph didn't – although I think he does now – was that pissing around wouldn't get you anywhere. If you want the nice things that come with being an elite boxer, you have to do the work that comes with being an elite boxer. And you have to be willing to do it day after day after fucking day. Joseph blew hot and cold, and that was never enough.

YOU DON'T GET WHAT YOU WISH FOR, YOU GET WHAT YOU WORK FOR

There's nowhere to hide in the ring. Boxing isn't a sport, it's not a business, it's a way of life. You can't fuck about with it. It's not something you can pick up, drop and then go back and pick it up again later on. It's not something that you can half do. You can't cheat your way through it. It'll always find you out. Always. I promise you. So you have to live it. It's got to come before anything. You have to give it everything you've got. It's more important than family, friends, birthdays, Christmases, it doesn't matter. If you don't do it right, it'll get you.

That's why sacrifice, dedication, perseverance are the most important traits to have as a professional fighter. Pure skill and a brilliant boxing IQ clearly give you an advantage, but if your legs are fucked after two rounds, then they very quickly stop being relevant.

I made sure that I worked harder than every single other fighter, because I knew how much ground I had to cover. Lots of people say things like that. I meant it. It's the same ethic that separates Cristiano Ronaldo from all of the others. He's not only fantastically gifted, but he's also fanatically driven, and that's the reason he's able to stay on a plateau with Messi: he works so hard and the others just don't. That's the top and bottom of it.

Hard work will always be rewarded. Hard work is what makes you better at your job, hard work is what makes your relationships better, hard work is how you learn and grow. How long are you willing to suffer for what you want? The ability to keep going when everyone else is done, to keep running, to keep fighting, is earned where nobody sees it. Nobody makes it to the top of their field just because they're lucky or clever or know the right people, although all those things help. The surest foundation of success is hard work. If you want to achieve the goals you've set, whether they're big or small, you're going to have to roll up your sleeves and graft.

WEAKER TODAY, STRONGER TOMORROW

I like winning. I hate losing. Whatever I'm doing, I've got to feel like I'm winning. Even if it's a shit game that no one else gives a fuck about, I have to win.

That was my mentality when I trained. When I worked hard and felt myself getting better, that was a victory. I might have been feeling exhausted, but I'd know that I'd done more today than I had yesterday. My mentality was: weaker today, stronger tomorrow. With that mindset, I was always winning.

In the gym we'd do something called punch stats, which is where you attach a two-kilo weight to each arm and then throw punches in certain combinations while somebody measured your output and endurance. I'd always beat every single other person. It didn't matter if they were heavyweights, middleweights, even featherweights. I smashed every record, every number, he had. I was like a fucking steam train. I'd just keep chugging and chugging and going and going. Sometimes I'd catch the coach looking at me as if he couldn't believe what he'd just seen.

What I knew and others never understood is that if you want to get to the very top, you can't rely on the gifts you're born with and it isn't enough just to turn in a good performance in the gym once in a blue moon. You have to be on it every day. You have to be willing to go out for those runs early on a November morning when it's pissing down; you have to be willing to carry on in the gym even when your whole body hurts and all you want to do is slump in front of the television and rest.

DON'T BELIEVE YOUR OWN HYPE

A lot of the lads I came up with were brilliant when they were eighteen, but then just stood still. They were barely any better in their twenties than they had been in their late teens. I think maybe it was because everything had come so easily to them, they'd never had that need I felt to get better all the time. You might be good at something. Great, well done. But there's always room to improve. And it's only by pushing yourself and leaving your comfort zone that you'll ever really progress. A lot of world champions win their belt and then almost instantly forget about all the hard graft they put in to get there. Instead, they relax, which never ends well.

I expect a lot of myself and I'll never settle or rest. I always want to be enhancing something and I never think that I've done enough. Which is tricky, because it means that I'll never be happy. I can't relax, ever, even when I'm playing golf. I might hit three or four good shots on the spin then one slightly bad one. That bad shot will play on my mind. It'll burrow into my brain and sit there, reminding me how shit I am, how I have to work even harder if I want to get better. My mates will point out that I'm just a beginner, and that even professional golfers hit a crap shot now and again. But all I can say is 'Not good enough!' Sometimes I hate being made like this.

But that mindset was also crucial to my success. The second you start thinking you're special is the second that complacency will take hold of you. And that's it, you're on the way down. That's what happened to me against David Dolan: I stopped to admire my own work and ended up getting chinned. From that moment on, my mantra was: don't believe in your own smoke, just keep going.

Don't congratulate yourself on being good at something – find a way of becoming better at it. Don't sit there being smug about all the things you know – remember how much you've still got to learn. Self-improvement should be a lifelong commitment.

DRESS FOR THE JOB YOU WANT, NOT THE JOB YOU HAVE

One of the reasons I was so excited to be on *SAS: Who Dares Wins* was because I've always admired elite soldiers like Ant

Middleton, Foxy, Ollie and Billy. Being around people who are at the top of their game is exhilarating. You learn so much from both their abilities and their attitude. I don't care whether it's cooking, cleaning or football, if you're in the top echelon of your craft then I think you're fucking great and I'm in awe of you.

My attitude during my career was that if you're always fighting people who are at your level or below, how are you ever going to improve? I always wanted to go up to the next level as quickly as I could, because I knew that just being in the ring with higher-quality fighters would elevate my own performance.

That mindset began when I was a kid studying the great fighters. I was hell-bent on reaching their level. And when I started boxing, that ambition immediately made me stand out from everyone else. It meant I was streets ahead of the people who were just there to look good hitting pads. I was thinking and acting like a professional even when I was an amateur.

At the Rotunda ABC, I was around the likes of Joseph Selkirk, Stephen and Paul Smith, Joseph McNally, Declan O'Rourke, all brilliant boxers. Being in their company drove me on because I fucking hated the idea that I might not be able to keep up. The same was true when I was twenty-one and joined the England boxing team, another group of boxers who were more talented than me.

Most boxers give themselves twenty or twenty-five bouts after they've gone pro before they start competing for a really good title. I just wanted to be pushed so much. I wanted to keep going and going and going, up and up and up, because I knew that my insanely competitive nature meant that I'd force myself to match the level of any fighter.

I barely paid attention to the journeymen I came up against in the early days of my pro career. I knew I couldn't learn anything from them. They were just there to scrap and swing. It was only later, when I got up to European and World level, that I really began to watch again. These guys weren't just stupidly fit, they were clever. Instead of swinging blindly, they'd be trying to manoeuvre you around the ring. Often they were little things, but they were so clever, and completely different to what I'd been exposed to before. Competing against them made me a better fighter.

All that is why I was Commonwealth champion and British champion within thirteen fights. That's why I fought for my first world title in my sixteenth fight. And when I got to that level, I never went back down. I never went for easy fights – I wasn't the sort who chose to fight a fucking crab every six months. I wanted to maintain the calibre of my opponent.

Whatever it is you do, whatever it is you want to achieve, seek out the best in your field. Try to work out what it is they do that sets them apart from the rest and then try to emulate it. This might be challenging, but I guarantee you'll learn a lot. You should never be intimidated by somebody else's abilities or accomplishments. If you learn to regard high-performers as an inspiration rather than a threat, you'll be giving yourself a big advantage.

WORK SMART

The training at the Rotunda ABC was so good. Far better even than the training I'd receive a bit later on when I started boxing with Great Britain as part of the Olympic programme. It was harder. It was more intense. We trained once a day, but we trained really hard. Whereas in the GB camps we'd have three, four, sometimes even five short sessions in the day and they were shit. They never focused on the things we should have being doing to make us better fighters. Instead of preparing for the kind of thing we'd face once we crossed the ropes, they paid lots of attention to stupid technical things that never actually happened in bouts.

I always bore that in mind in the years that followed, wherever I was training. There would always be a specific aim to the work we did in the gym. It's not enough just to monster yourself. Everything you do should be tailored towards helping you take another step towards that ultimate goal. You can't just work and work and work without a plan. If you turn up at a gym and start randomly working like a beast on every bit of equipment, you can't expect to get any results.

So before you embark on any project, whether that's

a triathlon or switching careers, make sure you take the time to identify areas you need to improve in or the skills you need to acquire. Then work relentlessly until you've overhauled your running style or picked up that essential technical qualification.

Don't fall into the trap of just doing the things that you're already good at. Be honest with yourself about why you're avoiding something. Whether it's leg day at the gym or a task on your to-do list, the thing that you don't want to do is what you almost always *need* to do. Cardio work was torture for me. But I knew it was essential if I wanted to ensure I wasn't immediately gassed in a fight. Don't work at doing what makes you feel good; work on what makes you better.

WHAT WILL BE, WILL BE

When the fighters I look after tell me they're feeling nervous before a fight, my message to them is: *relax, conserve your energy. What will be, will be. Have you worked as hard as you possibly can in the gym? Have you done all the mental preparation that's required? Have you got a good game plan?* If they say yes, then I tell them they have nothing to be worried about. At the end of the day, if you've done everything right, if you've done the hard yards, you'll climb into that ring and perform. If you've not done it right, if you've cut corners, you'll fall apart.

That's why I was almost never anxious in the dressing room. I'd be excited because I wanted to show everybody what I'd done over the past weeks. For thirty-two out of the thirty-four bouts I fought, it did all come good. Aleksandr Usyk and Adonis Stevenson were just better than me on the night, and I can live with that.

I know that a lot of people suffer from nerves or anxiety ahead of things like job interviews or events when they'll need to speak in public. There are clearly little tricks you can learn to help you cope with those fears. But for me, the surest way to keep calm is to know that I've done everything possible to get ready for that occasion. Anxiety creeps into your mind through the gaps opened up by a failure to prepare properly.

If you're the best man at your mate's wedding, you'll feel a thousand times more afraid if you haven't written or practised your speech in advance. If you're giving a presentation at work and haven't familiarised yourself with the facts and figures you'll be discussing, you'll be far more likely to freeze in front of your colleagues when your boss asks you a question.

Don't leave room for error. When you're on your way to an important meeting, work out your route in advance, give yourself enough time to get there, even if traffic snarls up along the way. When I was still fighting, I used to go out and look at the route from the dressing room to the ring, just to make sure I knew in advance exactly what to expect. It's not rocket science, but you'll be surprised how many people don't even bother to do these simple things.

One last thing to remember: those moments when you feel adrenaline rushing around your veins aren't necessarily something to fear. In the seconds before a fight, every nerve in every limb of my body would be firing. My heart would be beating faster. I'd breathe in short, shallow gasps. At the beginning of my career, I used to see it as anxiety. It was only later that I realised it was my body's way of telling me it was ready. It wasn't crying out for help, it was saying: *let's go, let's go, let's go*. Think about when you went on roller coasters when you were a kid – were you afraid, or were you actually excited?

If you can reframe that feeling as a positive, then what in the past might have hindered you will instead act as a kind of reassurance. You're going into war and your body has got your back.

SUMMARY

- You get out what you put in. Plan what you want.

- You can't cheat your way to the top. There's no magic trick that will make you a success. You have to work hard. It's as simple as that. The sooner you understand that, the sooner you'll start achieving your goals.

- Complacency is the enemy of success. Never think you've done enough or that you're good enough. There's always room for you to improve. Aim to end every day better than when you started. Endless improvement leads to endless possibility.

- Always try to test yourself. Take yourself out of your comfort zone. You don't improve by competing against people who are on your level. You get better by going up against people who are better than you.

CHAPTER 4
LIVE RIGHT, FIGHT STRONG

'Fuck, fuck, fuck.' This was not the plan.

We're in a B&Q car park. It's not long after 7 p.m. A minute ago, everything was almost completely dark. The only light came from the sickly glow cast by a nearby street light. But now everything is bathed in luminous blue.

I hear the thud the police car door makes as it opens then watch in the mirror as the bizzie walks, as if in slow motion, towards our car. It's me and a mate, and somewhere inside the car is a package containing something we really shouldn't have with us. Fuck, fuck, fuck. My breaths are coming in short anxious gasps now. Everything is going really well in my boxing career. People are even starting to recognise me now. But if that bizzie finds the package, and I can't see how he won't, then everything is going to come crumbling down very fucking quickly.

The guy reaches us and puts a heavy hand on the car's roof. Fuck, fuck, fuck. This is not supposed to be happening. I don't know where the idea comes from, but suddenly everything inside me is telling me that my only option is to run the bizzie over and then get the fuck out of there as quickly as we can.

The car is in neutral and my hand hovers over the gearstick, ready to put it in first. I start revving the engine. My mate looks across, his eyes full of panic. He can tell what I'm considering.

He implores me, 'Don't do it.'

'We're going to get nicked and we're going to go to jail. I can't have that. I can't have that.'

He's banging the dashboard and screaming now because he's realised that I'm still thinking about doing something insane.

'Don't do it. Don't do it. I'll take the blame; I'll tell them it's all mine.'

He leans over and turns the engine off. Immediately, the spell that's been cast over me is broken. As quickly and mysteriously as it had come, that impulse disappears from my brain. It probably doesn't matter whether it was my mate yelling in my face or some deep-seated instinct for self-preservation. The fact is that my hands move away from the gearstick and my body relaxes. The tension in the car slackens and we watch anxiously as the bizzie meticulously searches the car and – in another weird turn of events on this very fucking weird evening – fails to find anything.

I'm not perfect. My time on this earth has been full of fucking dumb choices. I've done stupid things. I've done dangerous things. So if you think that there's something strange about me sitting here, telling you that you have to live your life right, then it's only because I know how easily everything could have gone very, very wrong. I've made those mistakes and I don't want anyone to have to repeat them.

I sometimes think about the lads I knocked about with when I was a kid. We'd play football at the youth centre, go round to each other's houses. I think about what's happened to me in the decades since and what's happened to them. Most of all, I think about how their fate could have been mine. I wouldn't have needed to take too many more wrong turns or make too many more mistakes.

One of those boys has been done for murder. Another went on to become a gangland assassin with a big number of bodies to his name. He's now doing life. Some have been shot dead. It didn't need to be like that. A couple of them were amazing footballers and fighters who ended up deciding to turn down a different road because they thought there was no hope for them. There were others who never had the same talent but were still more than capable of making something of themselves if they'd been given the opportunity. Instead, they went out on the streets. Rightly or wrongly, they didn't feel as if they had a choice.

Things could have been so different for me. Those margins are so fine. If it hadn't been for boxing and wanting to impress my dad, I know I'd have ended up like them. If I hadn't made it as a fighter, I'd be locked up. No doubt about that at all. My problem is that I've always liked having boss things and I'm willing to do anything to get what I need. It wouldn't have lasted long – I'm no criminal master-mind – but let me tell you, it would have been good while it lasted.

That temptation was always there. I knew so many people who were involved. Boxing entices men to its margins who aren't necessarily fans of the sport itself; they just want the chance to hang round with a fucking hard bastard. While my dad was still on top of his game, he was a brilliant person to have by my side. He was very wise when it came to people, so he'd steer me away from the real villains. But he couldn't be around me all the time.

The biggest problem was that at the beginning of my career, just before I turned professional, we were skint, barely getting by on my GB scholarship. When I look back, all I can think is: *you fucking maniac – what were you thinking?* But I was in a different mindset then. Rachael had had our first son, Corey, and I wanted to be able to provide for him. I'd promised her that after she'd had the baby, she'd never have to work again.

The problem was that there were so many easier ways of making money than boxing. I could make a bit extra doing work with some trusted family members, but I also had friends who were out on the street making proper cash. So, little by little, I found that I was doing unsavoury things to earn money. That's how I ended up in that car. That's how I ended up within seconds of smashing to pieces everything I'd built up to that point.

Everyone has moments in their life when they can see

two very different routes opening up before them. That night was one of them for me.

Afterwards, I thought about how much my dad going away to the big house had hurt me when I was a kid. I couldn't do that to Corey, and I couldn't do that to Rachael.

I knew that whether or not I was struggling to pay the mortgage, I couldn't do anything that would get me into that kind of trouble. If I wanted to make it as a boxer, there were people I couldn't associate with, temptations I had to learn to resist. I couldn't allow anything to distract me from my dream.

It was around this time that my dad was put in a coma for a second time. He got jumped by a group of six or seven men, who left him unconscious for two weeks with a bleed on his brain. At least, that's what I think happened. Some people know everything about those events. I don't: I've never been told the whole story.

Once he was out of hospital, his wife fucked off and suddenly, caring for him became my priority. We'd always been close, now we became inseparable. That was the first test of my new resolve. All I wanted was to track down and break the heads of every single one of the cowards who'd inflicted that on my dad. But I realised that I couldn't, because doing that would have ended up with me in jail; or bleeding into a drain somewhere, all of my limbs broken; or worse. I'd begun to understand that you only get one chance in life. I couldn't fuck mine up.

BOXING ISN'T A JOB, IT'S A WAY OF LIFE

When I was a professional, boxing was everything to me. Nothing came before it. Nothing. I'd wake up and think about fighting and boxing. As I ate or watched television or went to the shops, I'd be thinking about fighting and boxing. The last thing I'd think about before I went to sleep each night was my next fight.

Everything in my existence was geared towards ensuring that not only was I in brilliant mental and physical shape, but also that I had as few distractions as possible. And this attitude wasn't confined to the weeks leading up to the bouts. I tried to live right all the time. That's why resisting the temptation to go back on the streets was so important. Even if everything had gone well, even if I never got caught or killed, it would still have robbed me of the focus I needed to make the most of my talents.

You don't have to be as obsessive as I was. In fact, I'd actively advise you aren't. But whatever your ambition is, you need to create an environment in which you can perform to the outer limits of your ability. That means eating right and taking exercise, developing good habits and cutting out distractions, whether that's bad company or worries about money. If you live an organised, balanced life, everything else will follow.

LET THE ANCHOR GO

I'm generally very good at getting rid of stuff that I think could trip me up. No matter how much I love it, I can just walk away. And there's stuff that I've deliberately avoided, because I know it's not for me. I've never taken a drug in my entire life. I gamble about once every decade – and only on things I'm certain of, like boxing. (The exception is Boxing Day, when I see mates and we all drop £100 at the bookies on whatever we want.) It's not that I disapprove of either, everyone makes their own choices, but I've seen what they can do to people and that's something I've never wanted to risk.

I can't tell you how to live. And I can't tell you who you can hang out with or how to spend your money. That's all up to you. I can't make those decisions for you. I *shouldn't* make those decisions for you.

What I will say is that when you're considering doing something or seeing someone, ask yourself one question: Will this help me become the best possible version of myself or will it get in my way? If you think it'll hinder you, then you have to cut it out. That was the decision I had to make all those years ago when I realised that the people I was associating with, and the things I was doing, were putting me in situations that could very easily have undone everything I'd worked so hard for. And I saw the other side of the coin play out, too. A lot of lads who discovered booze, drugs and women when they stepped into adulthood saw their careers fall off the rails. I've always found it useful to imagine I was talking to someone I loved and respected. If I had to tell them what I'd done, would they be proud of me? If the answer's no, then the odds are that it's a bad decision.

Bad habits and bad people are like an anchor tied around your neck. At best they'll hold you back, at worst they'll destroy you by dragging you down to the depths of the ocean. Why take the risk?

YOU CAN'T UNDO A GOOD CAMP; YOU CAN'T OUTRUN A BAD DIET

A boxer's physique is both his greatest weapon and his greatest weakness. You rely on it utterly and demand so much of it, but it can also betray you. That's perhaps because we have a fucking awful relationship with our bodies. We push them so hard in training that we almost reach breaking point. Then we put them under almost unbearable strain when we try to make weight. And that's all before we get into the ring with a dangerous fucker who's spent the last few months thinking about how he's going to inflict insane amounts of damage upon us. You wouldn't treat your worst enemy the way we treat our bodies. And, if anything, we're even crueller to our minds. It's inhuman to be away from the people you love so much or to subject yourself to that much pressure.

112

What I mean by this is that being a boxer has taught me a lot about what not to do. I've learned about the importance of balance and becoming comfortable in your own skin. I don't want to go back to the crushing diets, loneliness and punishing exercise regimes that were such a feature of my life in boxing.

I'm not shredded and I don't want to be. Even when I've been at my absolute physical peak, I've never been in danger of being asked to be on the front page of Men's Fitness. That's fine with me. When I was a fighter, all the work I did wasn't about looking good, it was about getting into the best shape for the job I needed to do. I still feel the same way: I'm not interested in looking like a Greek god, but I do want to feel fit, lean and positive about myself. What's weird is that I didn't realise how many positive benefits there were to regular exercise until I retired. I'd always had a very functional relationship with exercise. I thought it was what you did to get ready for fights and was looking forward to enjoying getting fat. Except that I didn't enjoy getting fat. I actually started feeling pretty sad. I was used to that flood of endorphins that comes from raising your heart rate and I realised I didn't want to carry spare tyres around my stomach.

Staying fit and healthy is a long-term commitment. It's far better to get into the habit of exercising a moderate amount regularly to maintain your fitness than it is to alternate between sitting like a fat bastard on your sofa one month, then beasting yourself like a maniac in the gym the next. It's not good for you and nor is it sustainable. Eventually, you'll just stop.

That's why I tell the fighters I look after that they need to live in a constant state of readiness. I get angry when they ask me for a twelve-week camp. They shouldn't need twelve weeks to get fit – six weeks should be enough. *You're a professional boxer, do you understand what that means? You need to live a certain lifestyle. You should be in the gym, you tit.* You need to be in the gym all year round, not just the weeks before a fight. You don't go to the gym to get ready for a fight, you go to the gym because you should be constantly trying to improve on your craft as a fighter. If you need to shift ten pounds in six weeks because you've had a good Christmas, that's easy. But two stone is a mountain. You have to be focused, you have to keep that goal in your mind all the time, not just when it suits you.

I had a fighter recently who lied to me about his physical state because he needed a fight to help provide for his kids. He told me he'd been in the gym – he hadn't. He went under the lights on TV, looked dead classy for a few minutes and then by the end of the first round, he was fucked. Now, he's got to work during the day and try to cram his training in his evenings.

The same is true of your diet. Being a boxer can sometimes feel like being a member of a very violent slimming club. We spend our entire careers obsessing over our weights. I wish I could be like my best mate, who's a footballer. He can play every Saturday and then go out every Saturday night. I couldn't do that, because I knew how easily I gained weight. As a result, I've always had to be very careful to put the right things in my body. When I did really struggle to make weight, it wasn't due to the fact that I was fighting at a weight that was lower than I probably should have been or because I'd spent the whole time between fights sinking ales and eating chips. But I watched a lot of other fighters who'd eat like pigs, train badly and then wait until the last week before their match to get fit and lose the necessary pounds. That's insane, and it would have been so easy to avoid.

Frankie Gavin was an amazing fighter. To this day, he's still the only British amateur to win a gold medal at the world championships. We saw a lot of each other when we trained in Manchester and both of us were always fighting to make weight. I had to get down to twelve stone seven, and Frankie, a light welterweight, had to make ten stone. It should have been far easier for him than for me. But he made it hard for himself.

The difference between him and me was that he just couldn't control what went into his mouth after eight o'clock at night. He'd eat a whole bag of Haribo sweets or go to McDonald's and then convince himself that going for a run would make it OK. Of course, it doesn't work like that. He ended up cheating his way through, always convinced he was one step ahead of his body, until eventually it all caught up with him. He didn't realise that living right is about making a series of small sacrifices. And, if you don't, the consequences soon add up.

It's just like with exercise. You could swing between bingeing and then crash dieting, but it's neither healthy nor efficient. Instead, think about what works for you and your lifestyle. What's compatible with your work and family commitments? What do you know that you can realistically keep doing over the long term? Moderation is key.

HAVE A ROUTINE

When I was in training camps, my day was planned from the minute I woke to the minute I went to sleep. Every second was accounted for. There was barely any time even to think. Clearly, you won't need that level of planning, but you need some.

If you create that framework, everything becomes more straightforward. You don't have to make as many choices, because you already know what you're doing. It makes it easier to both maintain good habits – like exercise and eating right – and drop the bad ones. And it helps you to prioritise: you can determine in advance what your most important tasks are, and then give yourself time and space to achieve them. You're not juggling everything, trying to work out what job to start first. That's why lots of people who don't have a routine will tell you that before the end of the morning, they're already feeling stressed or anxious or overwhelmed.

I still rely on a routine now. It's not as full as it was when I was fighting, but it's still phenomenally important to my ability to stay sane and happy. I need that structure and discipline.

Boxing teaches you about your energy levels and what you need to do to sustain them. Everyone has different peaks and troughs, and everyone has different ways of lifting their spirits and stamina. Try to work out what parts of the day you find yourself at your most alert and energetic. Ask yourself what sorts of exercises and interactions drain you, and which give you that bit of a zip you need.

I build my day around a strong start. Because I'm used to getting all the emotional and physical benefits of training, I still exercise a lot. It helps to clear my head and raise my mood. That exercise could be training hard on my Peloton or just going on a long walk – anything that raises my pulse. My day runs better if I've got up and trained. If I don't, my life doesn't seem to flow right. I can't get started and my productivity falls through the floor.

Those little things might seem insignificant, but they're the foundation of your day and help to get your mindset right. If you begin each morning by procrastinating or mucking about, you'll carry on like that until it's time to go to bed. If, by contrast, you start with purpose and energy, you'll have so much more momentum, which makes it all the easier to resist all those little voices that try to disrupt your progress: 'I haven't slept well,' 'I'll do it later,' 'I just have to do this thing first.'

Along with having a routine, I try to plan my days in advance rather than just winging it. This means that I can get more done, as well as ensuring there's time to relax and exercise. If you're feeling really under the cosh at work, it can massively affect your overall efficiency. This is because you run round in a frenzy, mistaking energy for achievement. You need to work out what matters, what you need to do, and then you need to do it in the right order. What you could do instead is take a moment on your way to the office to list what you want to do most, and in what order. Remind yourself of that list halfway through the day. If you give your day that structure, it'll transform the way you go about things.

Once you have those goals crystallised, you'll be much less vulnerable to distraction, and it's really satisfying to look back and say to yourself: *yep, I got all that done.* Just the act of mentally checking off those items in your head is motivating. By contrast, if you're running around like a blue-arsed fly trying to put fires out the whole time, you generally find that you neither accomplish what you need, nor actually get to rest. When I work with people, the first thing I try to get us to agree on is what we're going to achieve. If they can't explain to me quickly and simply how doing something is eventually going to help us achieve that goal, then they need to rethink it.

MAKE YOUR ENVIRONMENT RIGHT FOR YOU

When I was in the mindset of being a fighter, I couldn't have nice things. I couldn't be surrounded by softness, because I never feel like I'm making any progress unless I'm also putting myself through pain.

In the days when I was still trying to make light heavyweight and having to get up at half five to run on an empty stomach, I wouldn't brush my teeth because I wanted my breath to taste like shit every step of the way: I wanted to know that I was out there struggling.

And that's why I liked my training camps to be as uncomfortable as possible. I might have been in a dark, cold, gloomy city in the north of England while David Haye was drinking protein shakes on a yacht moored somewhere near Miami. I might have been miles away from my family. But I *wanted* it to be like that. It was perfect for my mindset and my physical approach.

It was me just me, my microwave, my iPad and a double bed in a dingy room in a Holiday Inn Express that cost me £60 a night, breakfast included. Although, come to think of it, I didn't eat much of it beyond the scrambled eggs, because I brought most of my meals with me in Tupperware boxes. I could afford to stay in somewhere more luxurious and I even had the money I'd set aside, yet I chose not to. There was actually a much smarter hotel that found out the rate I was paying and offered me a suite at the same price.

The food was lovely, the room was beautiful, it even had a spa. I stayed one night.

I didn't want any luxuries in camp because I didn't feel as if I deserved them. I hadn't won anything yet. Nice restaurants, nice holidays, whatever: all that could come *after* I had that belt.

I'd be at the gym on Monday and Tuesday, come home Wednesday, then go back there for Thursday and Friday. It was a long fucking slog. If you told fighters now that they'd have to lead the life I did when I was in training camps, they'd just say no.

I had that routine because I knew that that environment brought out the best in me. I'd notice when something was missing, even if nobody else had: it was a bit like hearing a familiar song being played slightly out of tune. All of this was very particular to me – I wouldn't expect anyone to want to do the same. Spend time finding out what you respond to. Do you work best in a room by yourself or surrounded by the chatter of other people? Do you need to listen to music to keep focused or is silence crucial to your productivity? It'll be different for everyone, but creating the right environment is crucial to unlocking your potential.

REMOVE DISTRACTIONS

There's so much going on in the world, so much shit, that if you can control even small things, it makes a huge difference. For me, creating a mental space that's ordered and calm is as important as having a tidy physical environment.

Although, I probably take it to extremes. I come home every day and put my car keys in the same place. My trainers will always be in exactly the same spot under the stairs. As soon as I arrive at a hotel, whether I'm working or on holiday, no matter how tired I am, I get to my room, unpack my bag and put all of my stuff in the places it needs to be. It's a ball-ache, but it's also essential. It's a massive cliché to say 'tidy desk, tidy mind', but I do genuinely find that when I'm surrounded by mess, it's that bit harder to concentrate. There's always something pulling at the edges of my attention. It's only once I've got everything in order that I can really focus. I've always been that way with lists, too. The way I've always seen it, you can either fill your brain with crap or you can get the crap out of your brain onto a plan or a list and leave space to think about what you actually need to do.

Doing training camps in a different city to the one my family lived in was unbelievably hard, because it shut me away from the people, places and things that I cared for most. But this was why it made such a big difference to my training. I had fewer distractions, so I could focus everything on the task at hand. I wasn't bothered by all those things that were grabbing at the edges of my mind. I didn't have to make difficult decisions about whether or not to interrupt my day to pick up the kids from school or meet a mate for coffee, because I wasn't even faced with those choices any more.

Moving to another city is clearly an extreme solution for most people. However, there's lots about this that you could apply to your own life. Ask yourself what things are distracting you from achieving what you want. This could be small things. If you find that when you work you're constantly derailed by phone calls and emails, why not turn them off, even if just for an hour or two? If you find that you end up lost for hours down social media rabbit holes, then maybe consider downloading an app that can temporarily block them. You don't need to switch them off permanently, just for those stretches of time when you need to be giving everything.

YOU'VE GOT TO KNOW WHEN TO CHILL

I'd always just keep pushing when I was in camp. There were days when I'd go back to the hotel after having been tanked all over the place in sparring and I'd be so tired, and my body would be in so much shock, that I couldn't sleep. But I found it hard to admit how punishing that pace could be. When I called Rachael in the evening and she said, 'You don't look right, are you OK?' I should have told her that I'd been absolutely mullered in the gym. That I felt like shit, that I was going back to do it all over again in the morning, and that the thought of putting myself through this again was killing me. Instead, I'd lie. 'Yeah, sound, I'm fine.'

Sometimes I'd need saving from myself. I'd go too far and make myself ill. I'd end up with a chest infection, coughing up green phlegm. I finished at least ten camps on antibiotics. It didn't end there. I'd get frantic that I couldn't give in to my illness, so I'd still turn up at the gym. My coach would literally have to push me out of there and force me to stay in a hotel where he could keep an eye on me while I recovered.

All this is a long way of saying that one thing I've learned from pushing myself as hard as I did is that knowing when to stop and how to relax is crucial. You can't give everything during the day if you don't take the time to fill your tank at night. There have been times when I've tried to fit in an extra run or swim in the evening, thinking that it'll help. It never did. I always woke the next morning with heavy legs and I found that it affected everything I did for a long time afterwards.

That's why my performance actually improved when I learned to enjoy my rest days. It didn't matter if I was going out to the cinema, lying on my bed watching television (*Countdown*, *Tipping Point*, *The Chase*, in case you were wondering) or just going to a retail outlet and treating myself to a new T-shirt or pair of training pants. Making that space was useful not just for resting, but because it gave me the opportunity to reflect on what I'd been through. I could ask myself what had worked well and what hadn't. I could also process my personal interactions. If there had been a bit of friction between me and my coach, then I could analyse it: Could I have handled it differently? How could I make it right tomorrow?

And that's also why I'm embarrassed when I hear people boasting about how little sleep they get. For me, it's the same as if I heard somebody boasting about how little time they spend in the gym. When I'm tired, I make shit decisions, I lose my temper too easily and it's harder to find that motivation I need. No car running on empty has ever won a race. You've got to know when to chill.

FIND THE MUTE BUTTON

Social media has bent the world crazy. I absolutely hate it. I know that it can be a great tool for business, which I've used to my advantage over time, but in general, it's toxic and full of nonsense.

It's not real life, and you should never forget that. Nobody's showing the day-to-day stuff. You don't see anyone admitting that the baby's crying upstairs or posting photos of piles of dirty dishes. Facebook, Instagram, Twitter, they're all dreamworlds.

Of course, the bits of the internet you should really ignore are those people whose entire lives seem to consist of lurking around social media, trying to degrade or pick on people. They're only doing that because, really, they feel bad about themselves. Why else would you spend all day abusing strangers? You're obviously living in your ma's attic or a shed and you're just sitting there trying to provoke a response from somebody you've never met. Fuck me. It's madness.

I find it easy enough to laugh them off ninety per cent of the time. But there's always that 10 per cent who take it upon themselves to go after my wife and family. Sometimes, if they come at me and I'm in the right mood, I might have a pop back. What really gets to them, absolutely *infuriates* them, is money. If somebody thinks that they can get under my skin by telling me that I'm a fucking bum and reminding me – as if I'd forgotten – that I got knocked out by Usyk, I'll point out that I've got so much cash now that I can't even count it.

Instantly, they ping me with twenty messages telling me that I'm a big-headed, money-obsessed prick. 'No,' I'll reply, 'I'm just showing you what this fucking bum has earned. Look at this watch collection – it's worth half a million quid.' I'd never say anything like that in a normal conversation. I'd be fucking embarrassed to. Which I guess tells you everything you need to know about what social media does to you.

In all honesty, the best thing you can do is not engage with these people at all. I don't block anyone any more, because if you do that, then they'll think they've got to you. If you do want to stay online, then try to control as much of the spaces you interact in as you can. On Twitter, I've turned the setting on that ensures that when I send a Tweet out,

I only receive comments from people I follow. And I'm a prolific user of the mute button, which has to be one of the best things ever invented. If I can't see what they're saying, it can't bother me. Even better, you could put the phone down. Go for a run. Breathe in fresh air.

LOOK AFTER YOUR MONEY AND YOUR MONEY WILL LOOK AFTER YOU

I'm good with numbers and I can count money quickly. That's a legacy from two parts of my old life. The one where I was a trainee accountant for a bit and another that I'd rather not talk about too much. I've had to count obscene amounts of money in an obscenely short amount of time. I've done fifty grand in twenty minutes (although in those days I wasn't alone). Even now, I reckon I could count a hundred grand in under an hour.

It was quite a useful skill when it came to my fighting career. There's an astonishing amount of money in boxing. But so many fighters lose it all. That always played on my mind.

I don't come from a wealthy background. For the majority of my life, I've not had large amounts of cash in my pocket. It wasn't until quite late on in my career – after I'd become world champion in 2016 – that I started earning proper money. Which I think on reflection was a good thing: it's the people who become stunningly rich overnight who can't cope with the insanity that comes with that sort of wealth. Now that I do have a decent bank balance, I've no intention of ever being skint again. It's not nice when you don't know how or if you're going to be able to pay your next mortgage instalment. And it's fucking tough when you can't afford the operation on your hand that you need if you ever want to fight again.

When you're struggling for money, it affects the practical stuff, like not being able to afford food. But it also spills over into every aspect of your life. Worrying about debt or not being able to meet your mortgage payments stops you from sleeping, it damages your relationships with the people you love, it interferes with your brain when you're trying to focus on other things.

Financially speaking, being a professional boxer doesn't mean shit really until you get to the elite level. The vast majority of fighters live month to month, which is why less than one per cent of boxers retire from the game with money in their pockets. There's an uncertain fighting schedule – you never know how many times you're going to get paid in a year, if at all – and there's a lot of people waiting to take their cut as soon as the cheque clears in your account.

You're also at the mercy of your body. If you hurt yourself, you can't fight. And if you can't fight, you can't earn. When you're in a sport where both contestants are trying to destroy each other, there's a reasonable chance that one day something will injure you in such a bad way that your career's going to come to an end. And I knew I had weak hands – even when I was an amateur wearing big pillow gloves, I'd managed to damage them. I was always afraid that my hands might retire me before I got anywhere near a world title.

The first time I really damaged them was in a six-round fight against Phil Goodwin at the Kingsway Leisure Centre, Widnes in December 2008. I snapped the knuckle of my left hand after landing a left hook on his head. It was the first heavy punch of the match and it left my hand feeling like it was on fire.

It was the kind of thing that could have ended everything. So I was lucky that Mike Hayton, the best hand surgeon in the country, worked on it for me. He literally saved my boxing career. I'd never had a general anaesthetic before and I remember saying to the anaesthetist, who had no idea who I was or what I did: 'Listen, I'm not sure if you've ever done this before, but I've never been knocked out, so I don't think this is going to work.'

'Don't worry about it,' he said, 'it's going to work.'

'Listen, mate, I know that, but I get punched in the face, I *can't* be knocked out. So, do you want to put an extra shot in, because I ain't going to sleep off a bit of liquid in a syringe.'

'I tell you what,' he said. 'Count down from ten to one and if after you've got to one, you can tell me what your name is and what operation you're having, I'll give you an extra shot.'

'Mate, that's not going to be a problem.'

'OK,' he said, smiling. 'Lie back and relax.'

He put this fluid in me and I managed to count down to four . . . and that's the last thing I remember. The next thing I knew, I woke with a cast on my hand and I thought, *shit, it's been done, it's happened.* When I woke several hours later, the first thing I saw was my friend Gary sitting there on the end of my bed.

Everything had gone well, but Mike Hayton told me I wouldn't be able to fight until July – seven months is a long time not to be working. I had two kids by this point. I hadn't been getting enough fights with Frank Warren, so I hadn't been able to build up any savings. I had no other sources of income and a mortgage on our terraced house that had seemed reasonable when I took it out but now appeared intimidatingly large.

The six grand that you get paid soon gets whittled down by taxes and fees for your trainer. I had nothing left. I was thinking: *fuck, what am I going to do?* There's no pressure like financial pressure. You haven't got a pot to piss in. January is a long month for boxers anyway – there's no shows, no nothing. There are no fights on the horizon. I couldn't work and I didn't want to go back on the streets – as much as anything because I was beginning to be recognised in public. That financial stress was in my head constantly, like a drum beat. It's the first and last time I've had to borrow money from anybody.

Normally I'd have been in the gym trying to improve

my craft, but because of my hand, I couldn't even do that. All I could manage was jogging. I couldn't punch for three months. Instead, I got steadily fatter and more depressed. Time seemed to slow to a sludgy crawl.

I was allowed to start tapping in March, so I strapped on twenty-ounce gloves covered in extra layers of sponge. I was tapping and tapping and by the end of the month, I was punching, but without much confidence. In April, I started sparring. When I realised that my hand probably wasn't going to fall to pieces, I called Frank Warren and told him to arrange a fight for the next month.

Frank sorted out an eight-rounder against a heavyweight called Mathew Ellis, a bit of a showman who used to arrive in the ring dressed as James Bond – a costume that the ring girls would then rip off. He'd been considered a real prospect once upon a time – a 'great white hope' – and yet now he was a broken man who'd fallen on hard times. He'd gone from everyone raving about him to coming in as a last-minute replacement to fight people two stone lighter than him.

I couldn't afford pity, even if I was worried about the fact that I hadn't hit anybody for months. At the back of my mind was the memory of the way my knuckle had exploded months before. There's a world of a difference between the twenty-ounce gloves you train in and the ten-ounce gloves you fight in. There's no padding, nothing really, in the fighting gloves. When I hit somebody over the head with a left hook, I feel everything.

I was scared, I guess. Scared enough to let it modify my style.

In the fourth round, I caught him with a left hook, hard enough that I saw his legs do a bit of a dance. This was usually the moment when I'd load up, move in and take his chin off. This time, I finished him with a body shot: another thing that boxing teaches you is that a man's torso is a lot softer than their skull. It might have been a departure from my usual game, but it seemed to do the job. After I'd whacked him, he just didn't get up. I think he'd had enough. Afterwards, he tracked me down and gave me what was clearly some advice he'd learned the hard way: 'Don't throw it all away.'

I planned for the future a lot more after that. I worked out that the surest way to avoid finding myself skint again was to invest the money I earned into something that would pay me money, whatever was happening in the ring.

For me, houses were the way. The first was a terrace in Old Swan, Liverpool that I brought off my brother for £93,000 (he had the kecks off me!). I still own that now. To begin with, my goal was to pick up ten terraced houses, which I could pass on to the kids. Even if they were on buy-to-let mortgages, I'd keep chipping away at them so by the time the kids had left school, the mortgages would be paid. I kept chipping away. As time has gone on, I've far surpassed that. I've got over thirty properties now: terraces, shops, a warehouse.

I've worked my bollocks off for that money. I've paid my taxes and amassed a fortune that means I've created great futures for my kids. If I don't want to work, I won't ever need to work again.

We make sure we enjoy our money – there's no point hoarding cash for the sake of it. Don't overindulge, but treat yourself now and again. At the same time, I'm very alert to what I'm spending. You should always live within your means. When you have no money or very little, it's actually weirdly easy to do that. It's only when you've got that bit more coming in that you find that a lot more starts going out. You get nicer things, but you're also at the very edge of what you can afford. You also get accustomed to a certain way of life.

So while I like Rachael and the kids to have nice things, I was never going to be one of those boxers who got rich and just fucking pissed it all up the wall with watches and jewellery, or who was always flying first class to Vegas to drink with their mates. A fast life can soon get out of control.

I also believe that you should always be putting money away for a rainy day. Life throws so many curve balls at you, there's so much that could go wrong, that if you can set something aside to help when times get rough, you'll be doing yourself a huge favour.

All this is a long way of explaining one of the most important things boxing has taught me. We all have such a twisted relationship with money. It's essential for our day-to-day existences and yet it can ruin relationships in the blink of an eye. Having none can be devasting, but having lots of it is no guarantee of happiness, either. What you have to ensure is that money never becomes so important to you that it disrupts the rest of your life.

SUMMARY

- You only get one shot at life – make sure you give yourself the strongest chance of succeeding.

- At the back of your mind, if there are people or habits that you know are standing in the way of you becoming the best possible version of yourself, then cut them out. Be ruthless.

- Invest time and energy in finding out what sort of environment gets the best out of you.

- Integrate eating well and exercising in your daily life. Look for a diet and an exercise regime that you can sustain over the long term, not just in short bursts. Moderation is key.

- Find a daily routine that works for you.

- Social media can be poison – don't be afraid of using the mute button.

- Money worries can become a huge distraction. Cultivate a reasonable, balanced relationship with money. Don't live beyond your means, but try to enjoy your money, too. If you don't put the effort into saving and managing it, you won't be able to enjoy it. There's no pleasure in spending money if you're too afraid to check your bank balance.

CHAPTER 5
ALWAYS START AT THE FEET

I let the footage spool on for a few seconds. On the little screen in the corner of my room I can see two fighters trading blows, each trying to manoeuvre the other around the ring. I lift the remote up, point, and send everything into reverse. Arms snap back to where they'd started, the men perform funny little skips as they're forced to retreat to their starting positions. I press play again, repeat the process. Then again. Then again.

It's 2002, I'm in the first, unsteady, stages of my boxing career and I'm so hungry to learn everything I possibly can about my new craft. I'll never be as quick or as strong as some of the other lads at the Rotunda. I know that. But I also know that my desire to absorb everything I can from the best fighters to ever grace the game will help me narrow that gap. The video I'm watching is from a couple of years ago, Félix Trinidad against Oscar De La Hoya for the WBC welterweight title – just one of the countless tapes that spill out from where they're stored under my bed.

I have never seen anybody move like Trinidad: he has so much coiled energy in his feet. He is like a panther getting ready to *spring. For the hundredth time tonight I watch Trinidad unleash that beautiful, vicious left hook. There's something hypnotizing about the spectacle. His tendons stretch, his body twists for a moment, then he explodes. I imagine doing the same when I get to the Rotunda, and the excitement begins to build in me. The nerves in the muscles of my left arm twitch, as if they share my impatience to get into the ring.*

Tomorrow cannot come too soon.

When I was a kid, there was nobody who loved boxing like I did. I was hungry for every single second of it I could get. Something that was easier said than done back then. Sky Sports covered the big fights, but pretty much the only place you could find coverage of the matches I wanted to watch was on KOTV, which ran on Channel 4 at half two in the morning.

I'd watch documentaries about the great fighters of the past or stay up until four in the morning to see Mike Tyson fight. I'd also buy video cassettes – there was a deal where you'd get three a month for £20 – which would show all the fights from the USA. My dad would fund things like that because it made him proud; it must have felt like a signal I was heading in the right direction. I know that if I'd have asked for the same amount for football subs, he'd have said, 'Behave yourself, lad.' By the age of fifteen, I had 200 stored in a big box under my bed. I kept hold of them for years – something that later on would turn my missus absolutely *mad.*

In fact, I only finally gave them away when I turned professional.

I watched all those videos over and over until some sequences became so blurry and worn out that it looked as if two ghosts were sparring. I can still see those ancient matches now when I close my eyes. So many of these fighters and bouts have been forgotten by the rest of the world – but they're still there in my mind.

If there's anything you want to know about almost any fight that took place in any division from the nineties, through to the millennium and beyond, I'm the person to ask. I know who faced whom, when and where. Fighting styles, records, everything. It just stuck in my mind in a way that nothing else ever would. My memory is shit, except when it comes to boxing.

I remember the first steps of great fighters who went on to become world champion. That's why I know the first person Mike Tyson ever faced – a guy called Hector Mercedes. I knew about Floyd Mayweather before almost anybody else in the country. I saw his bout against Diego Corrales – the only fight where Mayweather came into the match as an underdog. I watched fighters who should have gone on to be amazing, but for whatever reason crashed and burned; and others who fought once, lost and then faded away for ever.

I watched Bernard Hopkins, Joe Frazier, Britain's Johnny Nelson. Most of all, I liked watching Riddick Bowe. I think that was because I could see we had a lot in common. He was naturally a bigger guy, unafraid to raid the fridge. And, like me, he favoured fighting on the inside. Even though the rest of the world was always telling me that I should use my height and reach to keep the other guy away, there was always a moment when I'd think: *fuck that, let's have a fight.* And I'd get up close and dig them in the body. That came from Bowe.

The other person I wanted to emulate was Bernard Hopkins, who was the absolute master at studying, and then destroying, his opponents. By the time he faced Félix Trinidad in 2001 – the first big boxing event after the Twin Towers – the fucker knew every move his opponent would make. Hopkins said that when he fought Trinidad, he didn't need to look at his hands. He watched his opponent's feet and they'd tell him where the next punch was coming from. It blew my mind that Hopkins was able to break down an amazing fighter like that. It also made me realise how much I needed and wanted to learn.

Most of all, it changed the way I watched boxing. Lots of people watch matches and if they see blood and punches, they'll be happy. I loved that, but I was also obsessed with the details. Even before I'd ever set foot in a gym, I'd be alert to certain things: how were their feet moving? How were their hands moving? What did they do with their heads when they got punched?

Everyone else would be saying 'Did you see that cut?' And I'd say to myself: 'What are they watching? They're not seeing what he's just done with his feet, stepping back six inches so that he can then come back from the side and whack him. You were looking at the right hand that landed; I was looking at how he set it up.'

Piece by piece, I started to break down the men I saw on my little television. I'd watch the best fighters to see their strengths and flaws, how they reacted in particular situations, the sorts of mistakes they habitually made. I'd look for signs of what they'd do when they panicked, what they'd do when they got hit with a hard shot. After a while, it got to the point where I could tell within a minute if a fighter was any good.

I'd always start at the feet, because I understood that footwork is the key to almost everything. If you study a boxer's feet closely, you'll see everything. They'll let you know what he's going to do when he's been hurt or is under pressure. They'll let you know what he's doing when he's confident and looking to attack. They'll give an indication of their intentions: how is he trying to manoeuvre you? Is he looking to corner you? Is he trying to set traps?

Then, once I actually started fighting myself, I did everything I could to replicate what I'd seen on my screen. It might be a boxer's movements, or the way he placed punches, or how he used time. When I saw how efficient Lennox Lewis was with his jab, I started to copy it. And it was watching Félix Trinidad who made me change the way I fought.

Félix Trinidad was one of the greatest fighters of his era. I used to idolise watching him throw a left hook; there was something so special about it: a murderous combination of speed and grace. And nobody who was fighting at the same time as him, apart from Mike Tyson, could match it. I watched the way he always kept his right heel just off the floor, like he were a track runner. Other fighters are usually flat-footed the whole time that they're in the ring, but Trinidad gave the impression that he was about to start sprinting at any moment. Before long, I found I was doing the same.

I knew the game inside out. It was the only thing in the world I truly understood. When I watch boxing, my mind ticks and races. It lets me know that I'm not thick. Even now, if you were to give me a fighter, any fighter in the world, even if he's undefeated, and you let me study him over three fights, I'd be able to break him down and tell you how to beat him. I'm not telling you I *would* beat him, but a hundred times out of a hundred, I'd back myself to identify the style that *could* beat him.

It's a hard skill to pass on. Lots of the fighters coming through now aren't willing to put that sort of homework in, and yet that ability to watch and learn and plan was absolutely key to my career. There were very few times when I went into a fight without having a very clear idea of my opponent's specific strengths and weaknesses. In turn, this meant that I also had a very clear idea of how I'd go about beating them. My boxing IQ was one of the things that allowed me to beat fighters who, on paper, should have demolished me. It was also something that helped me to

140

stay calm when everything else around me was threatening to go off the rails.

My September 2012 Alexandra Palace bout against the Colombian Edison Miranda, for the WBC International title, came at a time in my career when I was feeling insane amounts of pressure. There was so much going on in the background that it was sometimes hard to keep my focus on boxing.

Less than a year before, in October 2011, I'd lost for the first time as a professional, against Nathan Cleverly for the WBO light heavyweight title. I actually thought I'd done enough to win, but the judges didn't agree. So that was that. I hated losing, and I hated even more that he ran his mouth off afterwards, claiming that he'd not even had to get out of second gear, that it had been far too easy. In truth, he'd told me immediately afterwards that it was the hardest scrap he'd ever been in. I thought he was a lying scumbag and yet, that couldn't change the fact my record had a blemish on it now. And I was desperate to pick up a win that would help to put me back in contention for another title shot.

Alongside this, I was embroiled in a legal battle with Frank Warren, who didn't make a habit of losing in court. We'd fallen out over a number of things after the Cleverly fight and our relationship never recovered, so I severed ties with him. In response, he sued me, claiming that I was still contracted to his promotional company. What I resented most was that for months, until the claim was resolved, he'd withheld money he owed me and that he knew I was relying on. The sense of betrayal and hurt I felt stayed with me; I was feeling bruised and suddenly unsure if I'd ever be able to trust anybody again.

Although Eddie Hearn had started to represent me, the legal nonsense had made everything far more complicated than it needed to be. I didn't have a contract with Matchroom Sport, so if I fell short the first time I fought with them, it might very well also end up being the last time I fought with them. Everything felt up in the air and uncertain. All this contributed to a situation where winning my next bout felt overwhelmingly important.

I wanted to be able to show Eddie that he'd been right to take me on. I wanted to prove that I was a proper contender who deserved to be given a chance of going up to the next level. And I wanted to show the world that whatever had happened in the courtroom had made no difference to my ability to fight in the ring.

All that gnawed away at me in the weeks after I got matched against Miranda. Sky really liked the fight. We'd been scheduled as chief support to Darren Barker, who was going to fight for the European title, but then Barker picked up an injury, so we ended up top of the bill. This was exciting, but it also meant that there was even more pressure on my shoulders.

Miranda was properly dangerous, with a brutal record of knockouts. He hadn't become a world title contender by accident. The Panther, as he was known, had a reputation for having a massive right hand. He very rarely got stopped and had a respectable record against some of the best fighters in the middleweight and super middleweight divisions.

There was something about his story that made me wary, too. He'd been abandoned by his mother when he was only a month old and everything that followed had been a struggle. He was working full-time as a builder and cattle butcher when he was still just a kid. He'd been homeless and hungry. When somebody has overcome so much, you know that whatever you see on the surface, deep down they must be insanely driven. I could see that he was like me, somebody who'd never give in or give up.

It was a relief to be able to take the time to study him. I watched bout after bout until I felt as if I knew him inside out. Then Mick and I sat down in the gym and talked it through. Once we'd come up with a plan that we thought would manipulate him and punish his flaws, we worked on our game plan day in, day out. We talked right the way through the process, tinkering it as we went along until we were confident it was right.

You clearly can't plan for what will happen at every single moment in a twelve-round bout; there are too many things going on for you to exert that kind of control and as good as I am at reading other fighters, I can't predict the future. You might know what risks the opponent poses, but you can't be certain about how they'll react to particular situations. What you can do is evolve a strategy that allows you to impose yourself on the fight.

It was obvious that Miranda's right hand was as powerful as everyone had told me. There was no doubt that if he caught me right, he'd be very capable of knocking me out. I saw how he'd won fights with vicious punches – he'd broken Arthur Abraham's jaw when they fought. But that was allied to pretty slow footwork. This gave me an opening: I knew that if I could get my shots off, then get out and come away at an angle, I'd be giving myself a good chance.

What nobody had mentioned, and I'm not sure many other fighters had noticed either, was that his body was his weak spot. Other people had hurt him there – Lucian Bute took the wind out of him with a body shot, but I don't think he realised what he'd done, so couldn't take advantage.

Miranda's weakness matched neatly with one of my strengths. I'm a very, very good body puncher, even if I didn't always get credit for it. I'm six foot three, this guy was barely six foot, so I knew if I could keep him at bay with my jab and detonate my right hand on him every time he tried to get close, then I'd be sitting pretty. Most importantly, we were confident that if I just kept digging him down, using my superior footwork, he'd tire quickly. It might take a while, but after eight or nine rounds, he'd be there for the taking.

I went into the fight thinking that he was slow on his feet. Within seconds I found that if anything, I'd been too generous. I couldn't believe that he'd been fighting at world championship level for so many years. That gulf in our quality instantly filled me with confidence: I realised that when I did make the step up to the next level, where I'd be challenging for the biggest titles, I'd be able to compete.

In those first moments of a fight you try to get a feel for your opponent. It's then that you can see how accurate your assessment of them has been. Watching a boxer on-screen is one thing, coming toe-to-toe with them is another. That means that the relentless focus on the other fighter becomes, if anything, more intense when you're actually in the ring.

The first time I hit Miranda in the fight, I touched him at the top of his head. I didn't put much force into the punch. It was just to kid him. I wanted to see how he'd react. Boxers generally fight with one glove up covering their head and another lower down, protecting their body. But if you tap someone's skull, they automatically respond by rushing to cover their head, which leaves a gap for you to exploit lower down, if you're quick enough. As soon as I'd caught Miranda's head, his gloves both leaped up, leaving his torso vulnerable. The better fighters don't fall for those sorts of tricks and traps. That told me something about Miranda. Instantly, I sank one into his body. I could see that when my fist connected, he tightened up and stumbled back half a pace. *Right, you fucker,* I thought, *you've felt that.*

It was too easy, really. I absolutely took this guy apart. He was so ponderous that I'd pop him with a jab, then take a six-inch step out, and he'd be left flailing at empty air. Then

I'd see him pause for a second before lumbering forwards. He couldn't make up the ground, which meant that he was barely able to land a punch. So I just carried on popping him then moving away. The only chance he had was if I stood still. Occasionally, I'd nail him with something quite big in the body, and I'd see him take a big gulp of air and stiffen a bit. That told me my punches were taking their toll.

For most of my career, the ring was a refuge. Once I'd climbed over the ropes, nothing else mattered. It was just a question of getting onto the canvas and fighting. Whatever was going on in my day-to-day life would fall away: the injuries I was carrying, the damage that my opponent had already done, the stuff I was worrying about. Cuts, gashes, pain. I didn't care. All I thought about was winning and fighting. It was the one place where I could escape the rest of the world. That's why I loved it so much.

This night was different. The seal had broken and all the pressure I was feeling outside the ring was flooding in, pressing down on my shoulders. It made me hyper-aware of the danger Miranda posed. He might have been slower than an oil tanker, but I still didn't want to give him even a single chance to smash me with his right hand. My plan was to fight slightly within myself. I wasn't gun-shy, but I was very, very careful.

In the sixth round, I dropped him with another body shot. Normally, this was when I'd move in for the kill.

But instead of putting my foot on the gas, I stayed patient. When I look back at the footage, I'm struck all over again by how cautious I am. Every punch is considered. There are very few moments when we step in and start trading. I think maybe that in that match I feinted more than I hit.

Sky hated that – all they want is drama. Their commentators, who didn't have the first idea about all the things that were pressing in on my mind, tore into me. And yet I couldn't let myself be swayed by the desire to be a showman for the cameras. More than anything there was a part of me that wanted to fight with the same unleashed savagery I'd shown during my time in the amateurs. But I knew I couldn't risk it. If I'd have got knocked out that night, it could have been the end of everything.

I'm sure it was a pretty boring fight to watch. Yet, for me it was one of the most draining experiences of my life. My brain was ticking and ticking and ticking. That's fucking exhausting. It sounds mad to say it, but in some ways that mental exertion was as punishing as any physical assault. I was watching every single move he made, trying to calibrate what risks I could and couldn't take, because I knew that there was no margin for error. And always there was the thought of Frank Warren and everything I'd been through in court. Then there was Eddie Hearn: we had no contract, nothing to tie us. If I lost, he could walk away and nobody would blame him. It didn't matter that the fighting was easy or that I was a far better boxer – all it would take was one lucky punch smashing through my guard and I'd be done.

When, nine rounds in, it was finally all over, I didn't feel elation or excitement; all I felt was relief.

BE WATCHFUL

The closer you watch the world, the easier you'll find it to achieve your goals. Whatever you do, and whether it's in your professional or personal life, you should cultivate your curiosity. Make it a habit. There were definitely times in my career when I put my head in the sand a bit, because although I sensed something was wrong, I was afraid of confronting it. I was like those people who won't look at their bank balance because they know they're going to be upset by what they see. That's understandable, but it's only ever going to defer that problem.

When you get your head up and start looking around you, you'll find that you're able to spot both obstacles and opportunities earlier than you did before. And the earlier those things come onto your radar, the better you'll be able to create a plan to deal with them.

And if you acquire the habit of watching the world, you'll also have picked up the crucial ability to learn from your own experiences, as well as the skills and wisdom of other people. Lots of people make the mistake of thinking that because they've not had the greatest experience at school, they're not capable of studying. But learning isn't just about academic textbooks and so many of us end up studying without realising it.

I learned so much from obsessively watching the great fighters of the past while sitting in my bedroom. Look outside yourself to see how other people are doing things, because there's always someone you can learn from. Think about how many elite sportspeople borrow from other disciplines to try to get the edge, whether that's football-ers doing yoga to extend their careers or rugby players training their peripheral vision. When you're interested in something, try to find out as much about it as you can. Ask people for advice. Don't turn down any chance to increase your knowledge or improve your skills. You'll never become the best version of yourself if you don't give yourself the tools to get there.

HAVE A PLAN

I had a game plan for every fighter I ever faced. When I stepped into the ring, I always knew exactly what I needed to do and how I was going to do it.

It's so tempting sometimes just to act first and think later. You want to get things done, so why bother with the tedious work of sitting down and planning? But, of course, in real life, just winging it rarely works. In fact, more often than not, it ends up in disaster. You should go into situations with as clear an idea of what you want to achieve, and how you're going to go about it, as possible. Ideally, you'd also know something about the other people involved and how they might react to the situation.

The very act of planning can help to focus your mind. It gives you the opportunity to work out what things are important to you and what's dispensable. And once you know exactly *what* you want, it becomes easier to work out *how* you're going to get it. Going into a negotiation with a vague intention of getting a good deal is only ever going to be half as effective as if you produce a detailed list of priorities in advance.

Planning also helps you to think about what you're about to face in a structured, orderly way. We all have to do things that sometimes we'd prefer not to, but I find that planning can take some of the anxiety out of these situations. It's so much more positive and productive when you're contemplating something that might be hard or unpleasant to think about how you're going to counter it. If I knew that the next guy I was going to fight had a dangerous left hook, just worrying about it wouldn't help. But as soon as I started to think about how I could counter that punch, the problem began to seem manageable. It's not unusual to feel anxious ahead of a job interview. What might help would be to try to think about what questions you'll be asked and what answers you'll give in response.

At a time when everything around me felt really turbulent, the very act of planning for my bout with Miranda brought me a sense of calm. When you're thinking positively about the actions you're going to take in the future, you're exerting a small but significant amount of control over the chaos of life.

BE ADAPTABLE

I never faced another boxer, with the exception of Oleksandr Usyk, who was as adaptable as I was. None of the rest of them could out-think me. And yet every time I've gone in the ring, my opponent has underestimated me. They'd watch footage of my last fight and come away convinced – usually with good reason – that they were quicker or stronger than I was. I never came across well on camera. I look sluggish and clumsy. But what they missed was that I also had a better brain than they did. That I went into every bout with a plan tailored to exploiting my opponent's weaknesses and masking my own. That I don't think I ever entered the ring with the same mentality as I had the fight before.

Being adaptable, knowing that there wasn't only ever a single way of approaching a situation, was one of the things that allowed me to beat fighters who were, in theory, more talented than me. Someone like Edison Miranda, who moved around the ring clumsily but packed an artillery-like punch, demanded a different strategy to Nathan Cleverly, who didn't have the same capacity to hurt me but was far nimbler on his feet.

It's so easy to believe that what's worked once for you will carry on working indefinitely. Sometimes that's true. More often, it's not. Get as much information as you can about the scenario you're facing. Ask yourself in what ways it's different to other positions you've been in before and in what ways it's similar. Fit the plan to the situation, not the situation to the plan.

PAY ATTENTION TO OTHER PEOPLE

Watching people is a useful skill and it's one that can be reproduced outside the boxing ring. The ability to observe things closely and draw lessons as a result is something that you can apply in many different areas of your life.

This kind of watchfulness can help you to be a better partner or parent. You don't need to spend hours watching old videos of your kids or wife, like I did with other boxers, but it's not too hard to pay them a bit of close attention. If you make the effort to work out what makes the people around you tick, you can respond to them better, anticipating their emotional needs. If you're the manager of a team, conducting a mental audit of their relative strengths and weaknesses will help you to get the most out of them. Watch people carefully, look out for what they respond to. Some people are motivated by praise, others need a rocket up their arse. So you need to tailor your actions to match what you've observed.

The minute you get out of your own head and try to work out what's going on in someone else's is the minute you'll take a big step forward in your personal relationships.

KNOW YOURSELF

A lot of people I know who are most unhappy are also those most unwilling to tell the truth about themselves. There are fighters who are riddled with the most extreme bitterness because their careers haven't worked out like they think they should have. They think they deserved more, and they blame everyone and everything for the fact that they're stuck doing nine-to-five jobs. They've never been brave enough to ask whether or not they're living in a shithole because they weren't willing to do the work early doors. They never examined the decisions they took or the mistakes they made. And so they carried on making the same mistakes throughout their career. They'll probably carry on making the same mistakes for the rest of their lives. Do I feel sorry for them? Yes. Do I think the world owes them anything? No.

Pay close attention to what you do and say. What are you good at? Where are your weaknesses? Pay close attention to how others respond to your actions or words. As you do so, try to put yourself in their heads. You might not always like what you see. You might even have moments when you think, *fuck me, I'm horrible,* but that's why it's valuable. If you pretend to yourself that everything's perfect then, you know what, things aren't ever going to get better.

When you watch your own performance more closely, you'll have a much stronger sense of what's effective and what isn't. It's hard work in the short term that might end up saving you a lot of effort further down the line.

LEARNING IS FOR LIFE

My ability to study my opponents, pick them apart and formulate the plans that would help me to beat them was absolutely central to my rise to the top of boxing. The work I did with my head allowed me to make up the physical gap that separated me and most of the other fighters.

Cultivate the habit of learning as early as you can and then make sure you never stop. Remember that learning isn't just about what you get from books or are told in classrooms. It can also be what you see and hear for yourself. You can learn from watching somebody set a good example. My dad, for instance, showed me the right way to earn money when I was teetering on the edge of going onto the streets. And people can also set a bad example. The fact that my dad lost his shit in a boxing match and that pretty much ended his career was, now I think about it, a very good demonstration of the importance of keeping a lid on your emotions.

SUMMARY

- Pay attention to the people around you. The more you know about them, the better your relationships will be.

- Be curious about the world and everything in it. Watch others closely to see what you can learn from them.

- Always have a plan. Don't try to blag your way through life. Assess every situation you face and then invest time in coming up with the best plan to deal with it.

- Be adaptable. Remember that every scenario, every person is different. The same approach won't work every time.

- Keep a close eye on yourself. What are you good at? What do you struggle with? How do you come across to other people?

- Never let yourself believe that you know it all. There's always more to learn.

CHAPTER 6

THE MOST VICIOUS CREATURE YOU'VE EVER SEEN

James Boyd is a brilliant amateur. He's had over seventy-five contests; he's boxed for England; he's a multiple junior national champion. He's probably the best fighter of his age in the country. Whereas I'm 3 and 0 with a cracked rib that's barely healed after a three-week break from fighting.

None of that bothers me. I don't give any of his medals a second thought. The bell rings and I just steam into him. Feeling good, landing the odd shot, I'm really scrapping, aware that for the first time in my fledgling career, I'm really in a fight. It's close, but second after second I feel I'm getting on top of him. I can feel I've got more power than him. It's just a matter of time before I land the right shot and I beat him.

I get in close and he spits in my face. Something just takes hold of me. I bring my head back and then butt him as hard as I can. I'm still in a red fury when the referee grabs me by the arm and tells me to get out of the ring. I can't understand what's happened. I just want to keep on fighting. But it's over. My opponent hasn't beaten me – I've beaten myself.

Boxing exposes your emotions like nothing else. It can tear off layers of skin and leave you raw and vulnerable. It can make you feel invincible. In the ring, I've gone to the outer edges of what it's possible to feel. I know what it's like to stare into the night sky as every single atom in my body screams with joy because I've achieved everything I'd ever dreamed of.

But I've also experienced the horror of defeat and its crushing aftermath: crying alone in a hotel room because it seems that everything is fucked and the world is laughing at me. The feeling that nothing will ever be right again. I've experienced hatred so pure that all I've wanted is to be given the chance to turn another man's face into a mess of pouring blood and jagged bone; and I've felt a surge of tenderness so strong it almost undid me as I stood over the unconscious body of a man whom only seconds before I'd been trying to destroy. I've felt a fierce desire to win that's gnawed at me for days, weeks, months at a time, and I've also heard that soft voice that urges me over and over to quit.

Most of all, I've felt anger. People think that anger is a simple emotion. I'll tell you this: it isn't. Anger is why despite having small, easily broken hands, I was one of the game's most vicious punchers. Anger and a furious desire to prove every fucker in the world wrong is what drove me on. Anger kept me going in the gym when my exhausted muscles were aching and flooded with lactic acid and all I wanted to do was rest. Anger is what made me a world champion.

And yet, it's the thing that could have undone me, too. Finished me well before I ever stepped into a boxing ring.

Anyone who knows me will tell you that I've always been placid and soft. Too placid and too soft, probably. I was the first person to help David Haye up after I'd smashed him through the ropes. My own mother doubted I'd make it as a fighter because she didn't think I was nasty enough. And outside the boxing, I'm soft as shit. Most of the time. But I also have a switch that transforms me from a nice person into the most vicious creature you've ever seen. Cross me and in the blink of an eye I become a fucking animal.

Anger is a part of who I am. Maybe certain events and experiences have increased or changed that rage, but the possibility has always been there. It's something you need, coming from where I do. I grew up thinking that doing bad things to other people was normal. That's what we did. If I ever had to hurt someone, I wouldn't hesitate to use the absolute maximum aggression. If I was in a fight in the street, I'd keeping going and going until the other lad's jaw was smashed in and I'd knocked out all of his teeth. That would affect some people – I didn't give it a thought. I didn't give a shit.

And there have been times in my life when I felt as if I could explode at any moment. All the time, all day

159

long, every day, I have this sense that I could do horrible things. I can't explain it without sounding like a fucking maniac. I just want to be left alone. It often doesn't end well for people who have that in them. The time will come when you take things too far and find yourself facing heavy consequences.

For me, that moment three fights into my career was an important lesson. I'd lost my rag and that had been enough to get me disqualified. I was going to win that fight. No doubt. And my temper had got the better of me. As had Boyd. He was a clever kid and he'd used all of his experience to get a reaction from me.

I didn't dwell on what had happened. I couldn't change it, so overthinking my reactions wouldn't have achieved anything. And nor did I come away thinking that I somehow had to cut away that part of my personality. I just let it ride. I thought it was always going to be a part of me. It's only now, looking back, that I've begun to think, *fucking hell, lad, you were nuts.*

What that incident did do, though, was to make me even more aware than before of who I was, and what my strengths and weaknesses were. I came away thinking: *this is me. For better or worse.* And I had to learn to harness who I was and what I could do. I didn't waste time with recriminations or self-doubt. I just asked myself how I could improve.

I was never going to be able to take that part of me away. For one thing, I realised that it was part of my appeal. The rage is what made people want to see me fight. Which is fucked up if you think about it.

More than that, it's what gave me the edge I needed to become world champion. I'm like many other sportsmen – if you take that element away, I'd have been a very different and probably less successful athlete. Roy Keane or Wayne Rooney were unbelievably gifted football players, but what made them special, what gave them that edge that turned them from being merely very good to being world-class was that viciousness. They both did things that got them into lots of trouble. But they were only in a position to be in that trouble in the first place because of that nasty streak they had.

I probably could have found ways to erase my anger so that it no longer had any place in my existence. I probably could have had it cut out like it were a tumour. Instead, I chose to keep it. I acknowledged its existence and learned to harness it. Because I knew that if I didn't find a way of exerting a measure of control over my rage, then it'd run riot and rule over me.

Boxing gave that rage a home. It meant that the anger that might have destroyed my life could be diverted into a passion that helped me to build an existence for my family that otherwise would never have been possible. If I'd been leading the life my friends had – working Monday to Friday, living for the weekend – rather than dedicating myself to the sport, then I guarantee I'd have hurt somebody really

161

badly and that would have only ended one way: a long spell in jail.

In the time before my boxing career had really got going, I'd had lots of fights and there were close shaves. Me and the Liverpool nightlife was a relationship that would have ended badly. I was arrested twice and on both occasions, the only thing that saved me was that I'd acted in self-defence. I left one guy in hospital after a rugby team attacked us while I was on a GB boxing trip. The last thing I'd seen, before I was taken to spend sixteen hours in a cell, was a man asleep on the floor with blood coming out of his ears.

It hasn't been easy and I've made too many mistakes to mention along the way. However, over time, I was able to evolve ways of managing that element of my personality. It means that I'm so much more in control of what I'm doing now.

I've always been Anthony to the people who are closest to me, who really know me. Other people might have called me Bellew or Bomber. But one of the first steps I took when boxing became really serious for me was to create Tony Bellew. Tony Bellew isn't afraid of anything. He could kill somebody without giving it a second thought. Tony Bellew does exactly what he wants, whenever he wants, to whom he wants. He doesn't give a fuck.

He was fuelled by the memories and emotions I usually kept locked away. The existence of Tony Bellew meant I could channel all of my frustration and hate into an alter ego that I'd step into when I needed him and step out of whenever I returned to my family home.

I'd turn into Tony as soon as I walked through the doors of a boxing gym. I'd become horrible – want to kill the world. When I was Tony, I was vicious and nasty. I'd have mad shit coursing through my mind. Having that ability to turn my anger on and off was central to my success. Without it, I'd never have been able to maintain my equilibrium in the high-stakes, high-pressure world of professional boxing.

It wasn't a perfect tool – I could sometimes lose my shit at the worst possible moment and there were times when I found that while it was easy to switch Tony Bellew on, it could be much harder to turn him off. There was more than one post-match press conference where I'd be sitting there, being asked questions about the fight, and I'd still have that blood lust in me. But most of the time it worked. And it was during the weeks before a fight that being able to become Tony Bellew was most crucial.

The moment I was scheduled to fight someone, I'd slip into street mentality. And that's what I'd keep with me every step of the way. I needed it because that time before a bout is full of overwhelming emotions. Just being in camp makes you nasty. It makes you horrible, it makes you want to kill your opponent. And as week follows week, it only intensifies.

In the first days it's all laughs and smiles. 'All right, lads, what's happening?' I'm back in the mix, I've got my coach with me again, and I'm excited and happy. Come week six, I want to knock him out, as well. Come week seven, I'm not happy. My trips to the camp are more intense and I'm angry all the time. Come week ten, I don't even want to look at anyone. Everything has shrunk to one vicious ambition: I want to annihilate my opponent.

And then come the last two weeks, when your body is flooded with so much testosterone and adrenaline, it feels as if you're existing on a sawed edge. At any single second you could veer wildly from despair to exaltation to the purest, most frightening rage. All of your training, everything you've been doing and thinking about for three months comes down to this short but intense spell.

At that point, you'll have stopped doing any hard work in the gym. You're basically just shaking out the muscles, going through the motions, rehearsing your fight strategy. But if your physical rate is down to a bare minimum, your mental rate is now right up.

This is the moment that you emerge from the seclusion of your camp – for weeks, your world has been reduced to your gym and your hotel room and the short trip that it takes to get between the two places – to find yourself thrust into the spotlight. People are questioning your motives, your aspirations, your expectations. As the days pass, the questions seem to get closer and closer to the rawest, most vulnerable part of you. It's like the journalists are probing for your weakest point. They know that your body is fine – what they want desperately to find out is how you're feeling on the inside. Physically, you know you're in great shape – you feel strong, you can sense the latent power in your arms and legs – emotionally, you're at your fucking wits' end.

When I saw the recent video of Conor Benn breaking down in tears, talking about how he'd had to tear himself away from his family to achieve his dreams and about how wounded he was by all the online abuse he gets, I knew exactly how he felt. I guarantee that ninety-nine per cent of other boxers would, too. They just never talk about it.

You see glimpses of that turbulence we're feeling at the weigh-ins and the press conferences. It's not scripted or put on – well, it might be for Conor McGregor and Floyd Mayweather; they ain't behaving like themselves – and all too easily it can go wrong. How could it not when you've got two men who for almost three months have spent all day, every day thinking about this fucking man who's going to punch their head and then there they are, taunting you. I've butted people, I've pushed them. Other fighters have kissed and slapped their opponent. Spitting, throwing tables. Before you know it, you've done something you regret. All of it is an expression of that pent-up, claustrophobic, confusing mindset. You haven't allowed yourself to step back and analyse the situation from afar. Instead, you get caught up in the hype and allow yourself to explode.

That's why I always tried to stay busy during that horrible last stretch. I did everything I could not to think about my family. I hated having to consider the impact that my obsession was having on them. I didn't like people even talking about them in the final run, because I'd be liable to break down in tears. There's a couple of times I've been so close to cracking like Conor did, and I was only able to hold myself together by closing my eyes and focusing on my opponent.

More than anything, though, it was in the hours before the fight that it was crucial to control my emotions. I needed to find the right balance between calm and the aggression that would always seize me as soon as I reached the arena.

I'm horrible before a fight. I'm *nasty*. At some point, it just happens. It's as if the man I am when I'm around my family and friends recedes and the part of me who's a fighter – Tony Bellew – decides it's time to take over.

I need this savage energy to get me through the fight. I won't punch as hard without it. But I can't spend three hours in this mindset. It's not just that it could all spill over and I'd end up lamping my trainer; although that probably wouldn't be ideal. It's also that it's exhausting being like this. If it went unchecked, I'd have drained myself before I'd even left my dressing room.

What I did instead was to try to break that time before the fight into thirty-minute intervals. The first part was about familiarising myself with my surroundings and making sure I knew in my own mind exactly what was going to happen. See it, look at it, believe it's going to happen. I'd wander

166

around the arena by myself, take a look at the ring, absorb the atmosphere as it began to build.

The next thirty was about complete relaxation. Switching off from everything around me. It didn't matter that I'd be locked in the dressing room, that I was metres away from the ring or that I could hear the crowd. This wasn't the moment to focus on those diversions. It was too soon to be wasting nervous energy on any unnecessary effort. I know lots of other fighters who lose all of their power in the minutes and hours before the fight. Their nerves have drained them before they've even entered the ring.

The thirty to forty minutes it took to have my hands wrapped offered a valuable opportunity to exert some control over my mood. It was a mechanical, almost soothing routine, the same wherever I was fighting. And it was calming to know that Jay Sheldon, the best at that job I've ever encountered, was responsible. I'd always get my left hand wrapped first, because I knew that this would be the first fist that touched my opponent. Sometimes I'd play comedy clips to relax me.

It was also a good way of doing my opponent's nut in. I'd get his entire entourage to watch me and my team pissing ourselves as we watched YouTube on my phone – stupid things like comedy clips or that video of the Man United fan losing it while saying 'give it Giggsy till the end of the season' – while my hands were being wrapped.

Like me, Lennox Lewis used to arrive three hours before his fight began. Unlike me, the first thing he'd do was find the bed he'd had set up at the arena and then sleep for an hour. Or so he claimed. I'm not stupid – there's no way he was stone-cold asleep. But if he'd closed his eyes and rested his body then it amounted to the same thing. And he wasn't stupid, either; he always made sure the cameras came in and showed him sleeping. If your opponent thinks that you're so chilled out that you can take forty winks, that's going to play all kinds of crazy shit with his thoughts.

Then it would change again. The minute the boxing board and the WBC had signed the wrapping off and the other guy's entourage had left the room, I'd say, 'It's time to go to work.'

I'd put my low blow on and instantly the levels in the room would go up. The last sixty minutes was completely different. It was kill or be killed. Simple as that. People might not want to hear that. It's not the kind of aggression that anybody wants to see in their day-to-day lives.

In the final stretch, the twenty minutes before I'm due to fight, I'm pounding the pads with my coach, the music pumping so loud that nobody can hear a thing. I basically think that unless it's rearranging the internal organs of everybody in a fifty-metre radius, it's not loud enough.

Music has been one of the biggest things in my life. When I'm driving my car, you'll hear me from ten miles off. Anywhere I'm going, I've got headphones on. It can trigger me. It can calm me down. It can make me smile. It can make me laugh. It can make me cry. Certain songs remind me of certain things. The lyrics will send me back to particular scenarios in my life, often my childhood. It makes me think of all the stuff I've done and haven't done. There's nothing that playing music can't draw out of me.

Music can take me to the most violent version of me. Music can push Anthony Bellew out of the way and bring out Tony Bellew instead. There was always one song – by Roscoe, from the *Training Day* soundtrack. In it, you hear Denzel Washington talking over a menacing harpsichord loop and a beat that sounds like a pistol going off. Its aggression and message were perfect to take me back to that place I needed to be. It made me think: *How* dare *you do this!* It used to drive me to insane levels of aggression in the dressing room. As soon as it started playing, it made the hairs on the necks of everybody around me stand up. Because they knew I was ready to go and kill someone. That nasty, murderous emotion lasted until I stepped into the ring. And at that moment, it stopped being a street fight and would purely turn into a science.

I was always in control of my emotions when I was in the boxing ring, because I couldn't afford not to be. In the weeks beforehand, that kind of anger was useful. Nothing was ever business – I took it personally every time. But while that pure, untamed aggression is brilliant for the weigh-in and helps to get you through the agonies of the last week, it stops being useful when you get into the ring.

Boxing is violent chess. On the one hand, you have to

keep in your mind the whole time the plan you personally are going to execute. On the other hand, there's your opponent, who's doing everything he can to disrupt your plan and impose his. You've been studying this guy, watching him for months – and that doesn't stop because you're stripped down and in your gloves. You've got to be so switched on. You have to be able to read their face for signs of overconfidence or fear. I'd watch their bodies for those telltale signs that they were tiring. The little involuntary sounds they let out or automatic gestures they made were big fucking clues to me.

Have I hurt him? Is he ready to go yet? Is his footwork on point? Is he sharp still? Is he just there to be taken? I know when another boxer is feeling the pace because they'll start trying to navigate around the ring, anxiously trying to avoid touching the ropes because they're tired and they realise that they can't afford to take any body shots. Most of all, you're always trying to anticipate their next move, because if you can spot what they're doing that millisecond earlier, you've given yourself a massive advantage.

I'd say ninety per cent of fighters will look at their opponent's eyes. I never did. Eyes give little glimpses away, but they can also deceive. Someone blinks and you've dodged a punch that never came. I was definitely someone who liked to trick the bollocks off other fighters. Anyone staring into my pupils wouldn't see what I was doing. I'd feint, make little sharp movements. And more than that, I've never been punched in the face by a set of eyes. I'd focus on their

170

gloves and then maybe when I was on the attack, I'd check their feet, see how they were positioned.

You've got all these things to process in your mind at the speed of light, all at the same time. You can't do that if you're seized by bloodlust.

You still need to keep your levels of aggression high; you still need to want to eviscerate your opponent, but you cannot let it get out of control. Everything has to be in the service of the whole reason you're there: winning a boxing match.

Then, when it's all over, that aggression and anger ebbs away. There's no other sport where you go from wanting to destroy someone to feeling a curious sort of love for them in a matter of seconds. That's not every fighter; the game has its fair share of vicious, nasty people. Some of them are born-horrible fuckers. But most of the time, I like to think I did the right thing.

IF YOU DON'T LEARN TO CONTROL YOUR EMOTIONS, THEY'LL END UP CONTROLLING YOU

Boxing has shown me so much about myself. It highlighted my emotional and mental weaknesses. I wasn't an emotional person before I started fighting. Coming from a broken home knocks that side of you; you don't want to give anything away, especially on the street. I never used to cry about anything. No break-up ever touched me. I was kind and soft, yes, but not emotional. Certainly not around other people. Boxing drew it all out of me. Until I went into the ring, I never knew how fragile I could be. And although I've always known I was a bit nuts – I can accept that because we all have a bit of craziness in us – it was being a fighter that showed me that I'm willing to go further than anyone else. It made me realise that I was willing to die in a boxing ring. I'm not proud of that but at least now I'm aware of it.

You're a human being, not a robot, so you're going to have emotions. Fear, anger, joy, sadness. Our lives are defined by emotion. Everyone will experience them differently. Some people might get easily overwhelmed, others might have a gentle, level temperament that's difficult to stir up. There's never been any point denying that I carry a lot of anger around with me. What I was determined to do was find a way of channelling that emotion so that it worked for me. Because I knew that if I didn't, I'd be at its mercy. The first thing you need to do, as ever, is be brutally honest with yourself. Work out what it is that provokes strong emotions in you. What are the patterns and the triggers?

The most important thing is to realise that not letting your emotions be in charge of you doesn't mean ignoring them completely or denying that you have any. It's about recognising when they're useful to you, when they're not, and behaving accordingly.

BUILD THE WALL

I'm a different person away from boxing. Anthony Bellew is soft at home. I adore my wife and kids. As much as possible, I've always wanted to protect them from seeing the man I became once I walked into a gym. Having the ability to 'become' Tony Bellew meant that I could establish a wall between boxing and my family life. I wanted to be able to display and use the anger I felt without worrying about what impact me doing so would have on the people I cared most about.

The other side of that coin was that I tried never to let thoughts of my family enter my mind before or during fights. Occasionally, there were flashes when I found myself thinking about Rachael. I'd wonder how she felt about the violence playing out before her. A couple of times when I'd been knocked down, the first thing I thought about was her and how I could reassure her that I was fine. It's not a nice thing to say, but when I was fighting, these human, empathetic emotions were exactly what I wanted to avoid.

My desire to keep those two sides of my life separate almost derailed me on that night in 2016 when I faced Ilunga Makabu. Normally, I wouldn't have wanted Corey (or any of my kids) within a hundred miles of the fight. I don't believe children have any place where people are likely to get seriously hurt. But this was different – I wanted him to see me crowned world champion. So I told Rachael that

I wanted him to be there but that I didn't want to see him. I'd been so emphatic about that. The arrangement was that he and Rachael would be settled somewhere safe, where there was zero chance we'd come into contact.

So when, a bit after seven, it was already starting to get dark and I was making my habitual prematch exploration of the stadium, I wasn't thinking about my family. Part of me had forgotten they were even coming. As Goodison slowly filled up, I walked up the steps towards the hospitality boxes, stopping every so often to turn round and look, trying to remind myself that this was all really happening. It was then, as I reached the top of the stairs and turned round again, that a high little voice from behind me broke into my thoughts. 'Dad! Dad!' I was so far away that I didn't recognise him immediately. I just thought, *that doesn't half sound familiar. It sounds like him, but it can't possibly be him.*

It was still so early, and I knew Rachael was planning to get her hair done and stuff before bringing Corey here. So it couldn't be him, I told myself. I turned round, convinced I was going to see a kid who just happened to sound like Corey.

Instead, my eyes met my ten-year-old son's and my heart broke. He was gazing back at me like he almost didn't recognise me. It was as if the rage and aggression that was coursing through my body had also taken his father away from him. I'd always seen him as the only innocent part of my life. I'd managed to shield him from so much of what had gone on around him – all the shit, nasty things I'd had to do just to survive. I thought, *you shouldn't be here*. But I couldn't say anything. I just walked away, straight down the stairs. I could feel hot tears rolling down my cheeks as I brushed past the crowd of stewards who'd gathered in the tunnel. On each of their faces there was the same look: *What the fuck is up with him?*

My coach had the same expression on his face when I got back to the dressing room. It's like the horror I felt when I saw my boy was still etched on my face.

'What's going on?'

'I just saw our Corey.'

Seeing Corey let all the anxiety and pressure back in. I knew that I couldn't allow him or any other member of my family to occupy my mind at a moment when I needed to focus only on tearing Ilunga Makabu to pieces. But it was too late. Other thoughts began to flood my brain: *What if something goes wrong? What if I get hurt?* My family were the only weak side of me. Just thinking about them made me vulnerable.

Keeping my worlds apart worked two ways. The boxing ring was also somewhere I could escape to. A lot of fighters over the years have struggled with their mental well-being. Often, it's stuff that's going on in their personal lives. Once I climbed through those ropes, I could shut down from anything that was going on in my life. There was some horrendous stuff – such as the death of my wife's brother – and yet when I was fighting, I felt more peaceful than when I was in the family home.

It's good mental and emotional hygiene to maintain boundaries between the various parts of your life, especially when you have children. I knew that my kids had to have space just to be kids. They didn't need all of my anxiety about fighting Makabu to be hovering over them every time we sat down for dinner. Equally, your job will suffer if you spend half the working day trying to deal with something that's going on in your personal life. If you let one seep into the other, you'll be less efficient and more stressed: there's nothing more draining or confusing than feeling as if your brain is in two places at once.

If you can set boundaries that determine where it is and isn't appropriate to express a particular emotion, then you're already exerting a crucial level of control over it.

TAKE A MOMENT

I know the temptation of letting your emotions go. It feels so fucking good to give them a good airing. And there's definitely a place for that. If you button everything down, it'll eventually blow up. At the same time, sometimes you have to acknowledge that your emotions can get in the way. That's what happened when I lost it after James Boyd spat at me.

But it could also end up being obstructive even in less pressurised environments. If I was in a bad mood ahead of going to the gym, I could have taken it out on the people

176

around me by being obstructive, snapping at my coach, refusing to take his suggestions on board. That can be satisfying in a weird way, but it's also pointless and negative. Far better to acknowledge that mood for what it is. Once you've identified it, you can try to work out what caused it. Maybe you slept badly or there was traffic on the way in. Once you can name that frustration and realise it's the result of an external event, you can reduce the hold it has over you. If it doesn't, try channelling it into something useful. Try not to get into a place where you end up carrying a negative mood around with you all day.

SPOT THE SIGNS

My temper is something I clearly cannot hide and that sometimes gets the better of me. All those years ago, Boyd knew it, which is why he spat at me. He'd realised that rage could drive me on, but that it could also sometimes lead me to sabotage myself. I'm never going to be in complete control of my anger. What I have got better at is spotting my early warning signs.

I know what winds me up. If someone unleashes a personal insult on me, I can shrug it off. I've got a pretty thick skin. But there's stuff I'll still draw the line at. I don't like bullies and if someone was to insult my wife in front of me or someone was to in any way threaten my children, I'd lose my shit. I could kill someone, no problem. And I wouldn't think twice about it. That rage is still in me. The difference is that these days it takes an awful lot to get it from me.

Be watchful. If you've got a temper like me, think back to the occasions when you've lost it. Is there a common trigger? Maybe it's when other people try to take advantage of you or the feeling of being stuck in traffic. If so, in future you can try to avoid exposing yourself to those situations. Or if that's unavoidable, it's useful to be at least aware that these events can have such a strong impact on you. It's all about honesty and not making excuses.

As you're doing this, you can also try to think about how your body behaves in the moments before the red mist descends. Do you feel dizzy? Do you grind your teeth or start sweating? Try to make a note of this. If you're aware of what your warning signs are, then when you next experience them, try to pause and assess the situation you're in as objectively as you can.

I have learned to recognise when I'm about to reach level four of my rage. That's when I know that if the situation develops much further, something bad will happen. When I can sense the blood rising, I'll take a moment to assess the situation and ask myself whether or not I'm willing to accept the consequences of absolutely losing my shit. Beforehand, I'd very quickly accelerate from four to five and there wouldn't be much time to think about whether or not what I was about to do was a very good idea. Partly because for a long time I *wanted* the chance to go to level five. This means that if, for example, I get into an argument with another driver and start thinking, *I just can't have people talk down to me and berate me like that cunt has just done. I'll punch your head in, I'll rip your fucking head off,* then it's time for me to take a deep breath before I do something very stupid.

Over the years, I've got better at reading those tense situations that could escalate very quickly in a very nasty direction. I watch the body language of the other guy and in the first five seconds, maybe less, I can sense what's about to happen. I'll notice when their back goes up, the moment their voice rises, the moment their posture changes or they clench their fists.

More generally, though, it's just as important to be able to recognise the signs of anger in somebody else as it is to be able to spot them in yourself. The better you are at it, the better you'll be at making sure anxious moments don't become aggressive ones.

USE IT OR LOSE IT

Anger can make you braver than you ever imagined you could be. It can allow you to tap into reserves of energy you didn't know you had. And it can boost your resilience in ways you might never have thought possible.

It's only a negative emotion if you let it be. If you can channel it into avenues that help you to achieve positive outcomes, you're far less likely to experience its dark side.

Of course, in order to be able to point your rage in the right direction, you have to acknowledge its existence first. Once you've done that, it becomes an unbelievably powerful tool.

In the weeks before a bout, I'd keep a screenshot of insulting or aggressive things my opponent had said about me saved as the lock screen on my phone. Every time I looked at that image, I felt a surge of controlled rage that drove me on through all the back-breaking sessions in the gym. My desire to prove people wrong by showing them that I could become world champion was another way that I could channel my anger into something positive. It was like a reservoir that I could draw on whenever I thought of quitting.

You're never going to be able to chase that rage away completely, so why not find a way of expressing it in a way that helps you to get closer to your goal?

CHILL OUT

Everybody goes through extended periods of emotional stress. For me, it was the lead-up to a fight. For other people, it might be exams or waiting to find out if you're going to be made redundant.

In those last weeks before a bout, I'd be thinking constantly about my opponent. I'd be asking myself what he was doing, whether or not he was working harder than me, what sort of mental state he was in, who he was sparring.

I had to learn to deal with that as best as I could, because otherwise, if that was ticking through my head all the time, it'd drain every last drop of the energy I needed for the fight itself.

I'd do whatever I could in that last week to take my mind away from what was coming. The first thing I'd do was reduce my exposure to any information or news about the other boxer that might not motivate me. So, for instance, ahead of my bout with David Haye in 2018, I muted him on Instagram. I didn't need to see what he was doing. (This worked OK until my mates started calling: 'Have you seen David Haye's Instagram? Fucking hell, lad. He's on a yacht! He's training on a yacht! He's sipping his protein shake from a cocktail glass.')

I'd play on my PlayStation, go for walks, go to shops where I'd end up buying some shit that I didn't care about, just for the sake of it. Anything that wasn't boxing. Having a routine was really useful, too: train, eat, eat again, eat again, walk.

This was never enough to eliminate those thoughts entirely, especially for the really high-stakes bouts. With David Haye, he was always there. I don't think ten seconds would go by without the thought of him going through my mind. Even when I tried to focus on nothing or on the PlayStation, he'd creep in somewhere. The only time I could keep it all at bay was when watching films. For two hours I'd be lost in whatever nonsense was unfolding on-screen and I'd be able to forget.

The worst for me was Nathan Cleverly – the only fighter I came up against who I absolutely hated. I genuinely didn't like that boy and in the week before our rematch, I was relentless in trying to get into a mental battle with him. Whatever I felt about him was returned with interest. Perhaps he despised me because he couldn't understand why a genius like him – he had a maths degree – could ever be out-thought by a mindless fat dope like me. Over the course of a week, I out-thought him, I outwitted him, I was cleverer than him. For all his cleverness, he had no banter or street smarts. I also found out what was going on in his personal life and I used it against him. At every press conference, when we came face to face, I'd look into his eyes and whisper these things to him under my breath. Pushing his buttons again and again.

I really got to him and yet what I didn't realise was how much energy I'd expended in the process. In the seconds before the fight began, when I should have been feeling sharp and aggressive, I was numb – completely emotionally drained. I had no snap in me because I'd let the build-up get to me that much. I should have had the power to knock him spark out, but I was too fucked to punch properly and the match degenerated into a dull war of attrition. Because I'd robbed myself of the chance to outbox him, I had to outwork him instead.

Whatever you're going through, remember that thinking about it twenty-four hours a day won't help. Your brain needs space to relax and recover. Find what helps you to escape – even for a limited period. Laugh if you can. Find stuff that amuses you. If you can have a giggle at times of stress and pressure, then believe you me, you can get through anything.

HOW BAD DO YOU WANT IT?

Everyone has bad days and everyone has days when they need a lift. For me, it could be when I was feeling shit after training or when it was time to get into the zone before a fight. I've always turned to music when I need to raise my spirits or boost my motivation – I listened to Whitney Houston's 'One Moment in Time' about forty times before my first ABA final. The other thing I find works for me is listening to inspirational speeches or moments from films. There's a guy called Eric Thomas, who I think is amazing, particularly a talk he gave called 'How Bad Do You Want It.' But there's also quotes from Muhammad Ali, snatches of dialogue from Will Smith films – stuff that speaks to me. I've compiled them on a motivational playlist that I listen to in training camps or in the build-ups to fights. It might be through my headphones as I travel in or in the dressing room, but it's always been there and it's always done its job.

Just as there will be times when you need to tamp down your emotional responses, sometimes you need to fire them up so that you can enter the headspace you need to confront whatever challenges are before you. Find your equivalent of 'One Moment in Time' or 'How Bad Do You Want It'. It doesn't have to be a song or a motivational track, it could just as easily be a picture or a memory of somebody important. What's crucial is that it's something that has the capacity to enhance your mood.

SUMMARY

- If you can't control your emotions, then they'll control you. It's as simple as that. Spend time working out which of your emotions affect you most strongly. Be brutally honest with yourself. Pretending that you don't have a problem isn't going to help you in the long run.

- Work out what your triggers are. Are there physical or mental signs that always precede an emotional meltdown? If you can identify these, you can give yourself a chance of avoiding letting things go too far.

- When you've identified that negative emotion, find something positive that you can channel it into. Try to keep this separate from other parts of your life. If you can set boundaries that determine where it is and isn't appropriate to express a particular emotion, then you're already exerting a crucial level of control over it.

- Everybody will go through periods of extended emotional stress, but you can't live in that mindset. Find activities that allow you to escape your stress, even if it's just for an hour at a time.

Nobody ever solved a problem by thinking about it every second of the day.

- Build yourself a toolkit that'll help you to alter your emotions. Find things that can lift you up or calm you down, just as I did with music and inspirational speeches.

CHAPTER 7

EVERYBODY HAS A PLAN UNTIL THEY GET PUNCHED IN THE FACE

The gloves you fight in at amateur level are like pillows. They're stuffed with the same foam that's used in car seats. Professional gloves are the same weight, but they're lined with horsehair. When someone's fist connects with your jaw, you can feel their knuckles.

First there is shock, as the concussive force spreads at lightning speed to every part of your cranium. Then there is the kind of pain that will stay with you for days. Then . . . silence. One second you can hear the crowd screaming, your coach shouting instructions. Then the next second: nothing. Your hearing just goes. You can still see the man who has just detonated a punch into your face, you can still think, but it's as if every single sound in the world has been removed. That can last, one, maybe two rounds. Six minutes of awful quiet while the savagery of the fight carries on.

I know all of this because of all the times I have crossed the rope and gone toe-to-toe with another man, all the times I have watched blood, my blood, spatter across my chest, all the times I have felt the bones in my hand break into fragments in the fraction of a second that follows the impact of a left hook on somebody else's chin.

Every punch I have taken, every cut that has burst open, every rib that has shattered: all of these have helped build my resilience. That is why I know that it does not matter that Roberto Bolonti has turned the two inches that sit above my right eyebrow into a sickening mess of crimson and ivory. I'm still going to win.

One day when I was a kid taking the number 79 bus home, a lorry smashed into us. I was on a seat that faced the vehicle as it exploded into our view. Seconds later it shattered the windows, covering our faces with glass.

That was the first time I felt what real whiplash was like. It goes right through your entire body. When I woke the next morning, I don't think I'd ever felt so sore. There wasn't a single part of me that wasn't drenched in pain.

I'd feel worse than that, far worse, on the mornings after I'd fought. After I beat Ilunga Makabu, I had a throbbing headache so bad that I couldn't sleep all night. At least the banging had stopped by the next day. It was worse with David Haye. He's got a way of punching you in the back of the head when he gets you in a clinch. It's like he knows how to whack you exactly on the most vulnerable part of your skull. He left me with a head that hurt so bad that it felt as if somebody was conducting a bombing raid behind my eyes. That lasted for four days, which worried me so much that I didn't tell Rachael, I just kept quiet. (Every time he got close during the rematch, I locked and tried to pull his arm out of his socket. He was saying, 'He's going to break my arm.' And I was saying, 'Oh, shut up, you bitch.'

There's no way I was going to risk experiencing that sort of pain in my head again.)

After a really hard fight where you've taken a lot of damage, you might find yourself pissing blood. When it first happened to me early on in my career, while I was in the shower, I was almost pleased. I'd absorbed so much of the mythology around boxing that I liked the fact that this somehow put me on the same level as the iconic fighters. I was less pleased in the aftermath of my first bout with Nathan Cleverly. He'd hit my kidneys with such force that I was pissing blood for a week afterwards. The novelty soon wears off.

I've had my brain shaken so hard that I no longer felt like I was standing up. David Haye once hit me so hard on my forehead that I couldn't believe that I was still on my feet. I couldn't even tell you how many times my nose has been broken. I do know how many times I've fractured or broken my hands: six. I've detached my floating rib and cracked my rib three, maybe four times. There have been gashes in my mouth, a cut in my neck (David Haye, again). My lips have been smashed open too many times to count. Oddly enough, almost the only things that haven't been bruised, broken, cracked or split are my teeth.

All this is a long-winded way of saying that boxers take a lot of punishment. That's common to us all. Even the most talented boxers will end up being given a shellacking from time to time. It could be that they've had a bad day or maybe their opponent just gets lucky and catches them with a fluky left hook. In a sense, none of that matters. The most important thing in the ring isn't *why* something happens to you or even *what* happens to you. It's *how* you respond to the setbacks you'll inevitably encounter during your career. What do you do when you've been knocked to the canvas, your head is spinning and your mouth is filling with blood? Do you meekly wait for the referee to count you out? Do you look up and try to catch your coach's eye for long enough to make sure he knows you want him to throw in the towel? Do you blame bad luck? Do you accept that your opponent is bigger, faster and stronger than you? Or do you fight on, no matter how much pain you're in or how much blood you've shed?

I would never quit. I have never quit. I'd die before I gave up. Nobody ever kept me down on the floor. I've never been left asleep on the canvas. And never once have I chosen to watch from one knee as a referee counted me out. Even when I couldn't get up, I still got up. Even if after I've dragged myself up, I'm walking like a fucking zombie, I'll carry on fighting.

I've had a gash on my face that poured out blood, so deep that it would make most other fighters stop. I carried on for another nine rounds. And won. I've had my right hand explode in my glove and carried on for five more rounds. And won. I've been hit so hard that I've collapsed face first on the floor. I got up and carried on. And won. You don't whinge. You don't complain that you've got a cracked orbital socket. You just fucking fight. Even if someone told me I'd lose my eye, I'd still carry on. Sorry, that's how far I'm willing to go.

That's boxing. That's the mindset you've got to have. You'll not get anywhere without it.

Roberto Bolonti was a short Argentine slugger, just a typical South American. We were matched up in November 2012 for a bout in Nottingham to contest the vacant WBC silver light heavyweight title. It was another step along the road for me, another step closer to being given a shot at a world title.

When I studied him, I saw what I expected from someone with his reputation: he was a rough-and-ready fighter who was tough without having that much skill. He was fast, could hit a little, but I didn't rate his boxing brain. He was rated in the top five of the WBC, which I couldn't believe – I thought he was crap. I watched him and I thought: *I'm going to smoke this fella.* I wasn't worried, even when he was doing all the finger across the throat shit at the weigh-in, pointing at his muscles.

My game plan was simple. I'm six foot three, this guy is five foot eleven. I've got the height and reach on him all day. I knew that if I kept touching him from the outside, he was going to fold in three, maybe four rounds. I'd start slow and then at the right moment, just blast him.

The first round was pretty straightforward. I was on top, controlling every aspect of the fight. When he came out for the second round, he actually caught me with a short left hook, although that didn't change anything. Not long afterwards, I knocked him down onto his arse. That was it – as far as I was concerned, I'd done enough now. As I came out for the third round, I said to Mick, 'He's not seeing the end of this round.'

The bell rang and I hit him hard. One, two and then boom! A left hook. *Fuck off!* The force of my blow sat him down onto the canvas and stranded him there. The poor fucker was clearly in shock, his eyes flitting all over the place as he tried to work out what had just happened to him. I thought to myself, *all right, I'm nearly done now.*

Then I looked over to Mick in the corner, gave him a little nod and went in for the kill. It was then, just as I was about to finish him off, that this cunt closed his eyes completely and swung a wild left hook that caught me just above the right eyebrow on my forehead. Instantly, it felt as if somebody was pouring warm water over me.

Bolonti had opened his eyes now and was staring at me like he couldn't believe his luck. Blood fucking everywhere. The first sign that something was really wrong was that my coach had been replaced in my corner by my cut man, Mick Williamson, who was staring at me as if he'd seen a ghost. His skin had lost all its colour. That's the thing about blood: it's scary when you see it.

I said to Mick, 'It's only a bit of blood.'

He carried on staring at me in horror. Eddie Hearn was in the front row shaking his head like he thought it was all over. Then I turned to Gary.

'What's it like?'

He looked at me and he went, 'It's fine, it's fine. It's only a scratch.'

He was saying this as I felt another splatter of blood on my chest and I thought, *fuck, that must be a bad cut.* Then I just thought, *Gary, you lying bastard.*

In the blink of an eye, everything had changed. One second I'd been just blowing this guy away, the next all I could think was, *fuck me, I'm in trouble.*

Before the fight, I knew that I could smoke him if I could get him to trade, but he'd spent the first three rounds doing everything he could to avoid that. Now, of course, the fucker was absolutely desperate to trade with me and yet I couldn't, because if he touched my cut, the referee would stop the fight. Bolonti was clever – he knew that if the gash had been caused by a head clash, the fight would have been stopped and I'd have been so far ahead on points that I'd have won. But because the cut was caused by a punch, I'd lose if the fight got stopped. Other people might have quit. Other people *definitely* would have quit. There was no fucking way I was going to quit.

By this time, Mick had gathered his composure again. 'Listen, just box this fight,' he said, 'and he can't touch you again. He can't get near you, but this fight could get stopped because of this cut. Just keep him away and box him and box him for nine rounds.'

Thank fuck for Mick Williamson. He's the best at what he does in the world. He'd saved more fighters with cuts than

I can count and had straightened me out numerous times. This, he'd later tell me, was by far the worst cut he'd ever had to deal with in his career. It needed twenty stitches: ten on the inside, ten on the outside. Another stroke of luck was that for some reason, a plastic surgeon was working that night, so he could stitch me up. If someone without that expertise had tried, my eye would probably have been a problem for the rest of my career. But you can't even see it now.

One last piece of luck was the referee, Victor Loughlin, a good man who never panicked. He was well within his rights to stop that fight and I'd have lost.

I said to him, 'Listen, lad, just give me every opportunity to fight. The cut's bad, it's pouring blood. I agree it's got to be stopped, but just let me fight and give me a warning if you're thinking about stopping the fight, because I'll go for him.'

I had to find a way to box through nine rounds – twenty-seven minutes in which I had to make sure he didn't hit the cut. Which was twenty-seven minutes in which the dirty fucker devoted everything he had to trying to get *anything* onto that cut. He was going for it all the time, trying to butt me, using everything he had in his locker to try to get the blood flowing again.

It took four rounds to stop the bleeding. I couldn't even let Bolonti touch me for the first two. As soon as the bell went, Mick would spend a minute squeezing as hard as he could, applying a swab covered in a chemical that would burn all the little molecules inside the cut shut. Then he'd fill it all up with Vaseline. Even after it stopped bleeding, it still looked huge and grotesque, like I had an arsehole on my forehead. And all it needed was for him to catch me there with one punch and the whole thing would open up again.

But he didn't get close. No matter how hard he tried, he didn't lay another glove on me that meant anything. A couple of glancing blows maybe. I just fucking bullied him. I was drawing on skills I'd learned years ago in amateur boxing – relying on my range and footwork to control the fight. By the ninth round, I was exhilarated by it all. Mick had done that good a job that the blood had stopped and I was making a fool of Bolonti. He looked like a novice trying to fight a really good professional.

He'd swing and miss and every time, I'd catch him with a body shot. I'd hear him make the noise that normally would be my sign to jump on him and finish him. That was my only frustration by the end. I couldn't risk it.

Afterwards, during the interviews, one of the security guards told me to look at myself on my iPhone. I caught a glimpse of my eye in a reflection on the black screen of my phone. All it took was one look and my legs went like jelly.

WINNERS NEVER QUIT, QUITTERS NEVER WIN

A good chin isn't about whether or not you get knocked down. No fighter is invincible. Anybody can get knocked down. Regardless of who you are, how hard you are or what weight you are, if another boxer applies two and a half pounds of pressure to the right point on your chin, your legs shut down and you hit the floor. That's science. That's just a fact. Everyone's button might be in a different place and some people will have a really little button while others a big one, but none of that matters. If you hit me in the right spot I'm going down, and I've got no say in that at all.

What defines a good chin is what happens *after* the fighter gets thrown onto the canvas. The question is: does he get up? I always got up. Every single time in my career that somebody knocked me down, I got straight back up again. As far as I'm concerned, when you get in the ring and you start fighting, you don't stop no matter what. You just don't stop.

A lot of people don't even know the meaning of the words dedication and perseverance. Times are going to be hard. At some point you'll hit a stumbling block. What you need to cultivate is the resilience that means you can just say, 'Fuck it. I'm going to carry on. It's going to hurt, it's going to be horrible, but fucking let's just do it.'

What's the worst that could happen? You might fail. Stick at it, be persistent, try your best. What I would also say is that I'm certain I wouldn't have got up if I thought I was just going to get up to get knocked down again. But I believe I'm getting up there to cause them problems. You knocked me down once, fine. But it's not happening again.

Because I've been honest with myself, I know my

strengths and weaknesses. I've trained hard, I've done my homework and I believe in my abilities. I know that if I break this fight down into pieces and I execute, I'll win. I know this because it's part of my overall goals – I know how each piece fits together into the thing that matters most to me in the world.

More than anything, I feel anger when I see people quit instead. I shouldn't, but I do. I know that they'll regret it, that it'll live with them for the rest of their lives. If I ever quit, it would send me insane. It would finish me. If I knew I'd given up, I wouldn't be able to look myself in the mirror. Here's a fact: if you quit, you can't win. You haven't been beaten by someone – you've beaten yourself. It's a natural law, like gravity.

THE MORE KNOCKS YOU TAKE, THE EASIER IT GETS

I've found that there's no correlation between talent and resilience. Actually, it's probably often the opposite. The greater the fighter, the lower the amount of punishment they're willing and able to take. They're not used to it and when times get hard, they really struggle. A number of the best fighters of my generation had brilliant careers but they never got to that point where they had to fight on instinct because their senses had been taken away by a cut or a punch that's sent them to the floor.

Whereas fighters like me who have scrapped, who have taken punishment right through our lives, are far better at coping when everything goes to shit. I've never been dropped sparring. Everyone I've gone against I've offered £1,000 on the spot, piled up in a gym bag by the ring, if they could get me to the floor. I've kept that money.

But I've taken some hidings in the gym over the years. I've paid a lot of fighters a lot of money to come in and knock the fuck out of me. David Price absolutely mullered me. Nothing went right for me in that session and he battered me for about six or seven rounds. Most fighters would say, 'I'm having a shit day, I'm getting out.' But it's in me just to take it.

Some fighters will see being knocked about in sparring as a bad thing. For me, it was all a positive. For one thing, I always knew that the most important thing was what happened on the night, under the lights; all this was just a dress rehearsal. More significantly, I knew that every punch I took, every time I took a blow, was something else that would help to prepare me for the shock and violence of actually fighting.

Those hard moments pile up over a lifetime. They mean that when you're really tested, you find that you're ready. You need to think about failure, not ignore it. Don't just practice for a job interview or a presentation that goes perfectly. Think about the one question they could ask that would really trip you up. Then it won't. We've all sat through enough shit best man speeches with pauses for

198

laughter that doesn't come. Hope for the best but prepare for the worst. Luckily for you, this won't involve you paying someone to batter the shit out of you, but it will have the same impact. You don't want to go through life with a glass jaw.

DRAW ON YOUR PAST

I've never been cut as deep as I was in that fight against Bolonti. But I was able to draw on experiences from my past to help me. It was here that all the years I'd spent studying the masters of their craft came into their own. I'd seen how the best fighters in history responded when they got hurt and knocked down. At that point it hadn't happened to me, but I kept watching fights over and over because I knew that at some point in my career, I'd end up on my arse.

Some of them were clever nuts – they'd just take a second, haul themselves up on one knee by the count of three and then see the rest of the count until it gets to six, breathe and watch the referee count. They'd wait until six or seven to give themselves time to gather their momentum and balance their legs, then they'd leap up all strong again.

All that watching went out of the window when I did get smashed over in the ring. No waiting for me, something in me would always try to get up before the referee got to three. It was like an urgent message in my mind: *I've gotta get up, gotta get up, gotta get up as fast as I can.*

Latest it ever took was six, but I'd always be up, wanting to punch the other fighter's face in, showing to the referee I was fit and able to fight. The referee might be a good one who lets stuff flow, they might not. You can't anticipate that and you can't take the risk of them waving the bout off because they think you're fucked, so you've got to be quick.

And there were moments from my own career when I'd been in similarly awkward positions that I could look back on. Back in 2010, when I'd just turned twenty-eight, I went into my first fight with the Jamaican Ovill McKenzie, a 10,000 sell-out for the British Commonwealth Championship, overflowing with confidence. I was the big favourite, 12 and 0, knocking the fuck out of everyone who crossed my path. It was one of the few fights in my career where I hadn't even bothered to do much studying. I'd watched him get knocked out clean by Dean Francis in one round and I'd looked at his record – 18 wins, 9 defeats – and thought, *this fella is just going to get eaten alive. I'm going to smoke him.*

Then this guy, this loser, came out in the first round and before I knew it, he'd banged me on the side of my head and I'd been knocked down on my arse. I got back up on the count of three or four with a pain in my head and an uncomfortable realisation that I was in the ring with a proper rival.

Not that this changed much. In the second round, he hit me right down the pipe on the chin and I dropped flat on my face. That was a heavy, heavy knock-down, the kind that's so hard you don't even know what happened. I heard a loud bang as his glove smashed into me and then it was like an explosion had gone off in my head. My legs went and then all of a sudden, I found myself looking down, with my hands on the floor. A single dazed question swirled through my brain: *What the fuck is going on?*

To this day, I still don't know how I got up, but anyway, on the count of four, there I was. I remember the referee asked if I was OK. I told him I was fine.

Then he said, 'Where are you?'

'I'm in fucking Liverpool,' I told him, just as he'd got to six. 'No fucking way,' I said. 'I'm going to kill him.' I started walking around saying, 'If you don't move out the way, you're fucking dead. I'm going to nail this fella. He's finished.'

The referee stared at me as if he thought I'd gone out of my mind – not the first time in my career that had happened and it certainly wouldn't be the last – and then waved the fight on.

That's when I looked into McKenzie's eyes. The second he returned that glance was the second he lost that fight. His face was a mask of sheer disbelief. He'd hit me with everything he had and still I'd got up. Later on, he'd say he was convinced I was on drugs. He'd started out working as a doorman, he said, and it was only people who were off their tits who could withstand that sort of punishment.

That was it. He fell apart. For the first two rounds he'd been fighting out of his skin. His speed was unbelievable, his power was unbelievable. All it took was planting that seed of doubt in his mindset and it was as if every ounce of his strength and agility had been drained from him.

It was easy after that. I just walked through him and knocked him out in the seventh round. This cunt had knocked me down twice in the first two rounds, he had all the momentum with him, he was fighting levels above what he was normally capable of. This should have been a very fucking good day for him. Instead, he threw it all away because he got spooked. It didn't matter how hard his punches were that night or how quick he could move his feet, he lost his nerve. That moment when he needed his mindset to be resilient, it crumbled.

The specific circumstances of that contest were different to my fight with Bolonti, but the thing that shored up my confidence was knowing that I'd been rocked by an unexpected sequence of events in the ring and come out the other end victorious. The very fact that I'd survived that sort of trouble once meant that I was confident I'd be able to do so again.

MASTER THE FUNDAMENTALS

In one sense, the Bolonti fight was a step into unknown territory. In another, it was just a reaffirmation of basic principles. I didn't do what I'd planned to do on that particular night, but I still fought in a way I'd practised over and over in the past. When I unleashed a punch combination on another fighter, I never needed to think about what I was doing, because I'd drilled it in me at the gym until it was second nature. It meant that I had space in my head for the stuff that mattered on the night.

Whenever I fought, I was always supremely fit. I might not have looked aesthetically great, but believe you me, I was in unbelievable shape. That's why whenever I got knocked down, I was always up at the count of six or seven at the latest. Other fighters stumbled because their balance is all over the place. I never did. When I got up, my legs were strong beneath me because of all the work I'd put into the camp. That work wasn't sexy – nobody could see it on Instagram – but I knew I could rely on it. Against Bolonti, I had to revert to a fighting style that I'd used in the amateurs. Again, it was an example of me being able to draw on fundamental skills that were ingrained in me through years of practice.

Never forget how important the essential building blocks of your profession are. Often, when things go south, they're the things you'll have to rely on. Whatever your trade, make sure you've mastered the fundamentals. Practise them until you can do them blindfolded. You never know when you might need them.

ACCEPT CHAOS

Sometimes your carefully laid plans will be exploded by a mistake or an unexpected event. Those things happen – you'd be an idiot if you pretended they didn't. As much as I'd want to dominate another boxer, I couldn't control every single move they made. Bolonti's shut-eyed punch was a fluke. It just happened to be a fluke that reduced my face to a bloodied mess. And nor can you control every aspect of the world. It's too big, too chaotic for that. You can control your reactions to the shocks life throws you and you can also do everything you can to make sure that when you do face those challenges, you're prepared.

Consciously or not, I was preparing myself for the possibility that things would go south. Don't get me wrong, I'd always go into fights thinking I'd win. But you have to find a balance between that belief that you'll prevail and an acknowledgement that times will get tough. If you don't have enough of the latter, you'll find yourself constantly surprised by bad news, which can have a devastating effect on your motivation. People who pretend to themselves that 'everything will be OK, no need to worry' are those who don't take the time to cultivate the discipline needed to confront the brutal realities of life.

So when you think about your goals, devote an equal amount of attention to considering the obstacles you might encounter on the way to achieving them. Think about what could go wrong and how you'll respond. That way, when issues do come up – which I guarantee they will – you'll already be psychologically prepared. You'll be able to put them in perspective: this is just a bump in the road, nothing more.

ACKNOWLEDGE THE PROBLEM

When I felt blood pouring onto my chest, it would have been madness to pretend everything was OK. Everything was far from fucking OK. Acknowledging that I was in trouble was a start. If I pretended the problem wasn't there, I was never going to be able to solve it. But nor was it a moment to wallow in self-pity. If I convinced myself that the problem was bigger than it really is – perhaps because I want an excuse – then I'd be more likely to be defeated by it. The fact is, while the cut was a setback, it was only that. I was able to put it in perspective and stay calm.

THE FIRST TIME YOU SPEW IT IS THE HARDEST

John 'Duke' Doolan was Jimmy's best friend at the Rotunda. He was never a great boxing coach. He was just a hard fucker who you could always rely on to tell you exactly how he felt. But just as we were preparing for the ABAs, he gave me one of the most important pieces of advice I've ever had. 'I'm not the best boxer,' he told me. 'I'm not going to tell you how to beat fighters. I'm not going to tell you how to do this and that. One thing I'll give you is, don't you ever spew it. The first time you spew it, it's the hardest. After you've spewed it once, you'll spew it again and spew it again. So just do me a favour and don't ever spew it.' That's stuck with me for ever. I never ever spewed it.

Duke had seen something. He always knew I had ability and he knew that I could punch like fuck. He'd also spotted that there were times when I didn't want to work as hard as some of the others or when I was so drained physically that I couldn't, and yet I carried on. For instance, we'd go out on a run or hit the circuits and I wouldn't be able to keep up with the other, more natural athletes. It wasn't laziness, it was because I was the biggest in the gym and my body struggled to match the pace they set.

On some days I'd force myself so hard that I'd be puking at the end of the session. The other lads would be laughing at me, calling me a big girl for being so fucked that I was emptying my guts. Duke was proud, though. 'He's not quitting, that kid.'

And I've never forgotten what Duke told me. What he meant was: if you quit once, you won't be able to stop quitting. It'll become a habit and the thing with habits is that they can be very hard to break. You can't afford to allow even that tiny crack in the wall, because before you know it, the whole house will have fallen to pieces. If there had been a morning when I decided that I couldn't carry on, it wouldn't have been a one-off. It would have been the first in a sequence of mornings when I spewed. That sequence would have ended with me drifting out of the sport.

I've never quit anything I've ever done. No matter how hard it's got, no matter how much I don't want to put my trainers on and get out there. I'm the same now, with my knackered old body and nothing to train for. I'll get on my Peloton and after twenty minutes, I'll just be thinking, *fuck this, I can't be arsed. My knees are killing. My knees are on fire.* But I don't quit, I can't give in. Because I know that if I do, the chances of me getting back on that bike the next morning will already be shrinking fast.

That's the attitude I always had in the ring. Even in fights when I've been getting outboxed or I'm getting outpunched and my face is fucked and my nose has been broken, my hands smashed to pieces, I just can't give in. That's because I've always taken Duke's words to heart: quitting becomes a habit – make sure you never start.

SUMMARY

- Life will throw all sorts of shit at you. You can't change that, but you can change how you respond to those situations.

- If you pretend that life is always going to be a bed of roses, you're setting yourself up for a big disappointment. Think about what could go wrong. If you can, think about what practical steps you can take if the worst were to happen. But try to prepare yourself mentally, too.

- You build resilience incrementally. It's not something that's handed to you like a new suit off the rack. Get out there. Every knock you take will make you stronger. Every setback you experience will make the next one easier to absorb.

- When you have your fundamentals sorted, it leaves space in your brain to find new solutions to the situation in front of you.

- When your back is against the wall, draw on times in the past when you've overcome obstacles or beaten tough situations. Knowing that you've made it through before will help you to believe you can do so again.

- Never give up. Just. Don't. Do It. If you quit once, you'll never stop.

CHAPTER 8
THE NIGHTMARE

30 November 2013, Quebec City, Canada

This isn't what I'd expected. This isn't what I wanted. I throw a punch at Adonis Stevenson. Any other fighter and I'd have felt a lightning bolt shoot up my arm as my fist connected viciously with his chin. But he's moved so quickly out of my reach that I'm left swiping uselessly at empty space. What the fuck is this?

His judgement of distance is incredible, a sickening realisation that hits me harder than his punches. He has an elusive, quicksilver ability to tell exactly when he's two or three inches away from me that cannot be captured in video footage. I'll think I'm safe, then suddenly he appears out of range and catches me with these hard accurate shots. Almost as soon as he's leaned in to smash me with that right hand, he's darted away again. It feels impossible to grasp him. Time after time I've attacked and yet I always struggle to land anything meaningful. It's like fighting a ghost. In the third round he catches me with a straight left on the forehead. There's so much power in his fists. I hear a sickening crack and think he's crushed the bone. I think: oh my God, he's cracked my fucking skull.

I just need one chance to land the punch that will destroy him. But my body is empty. I feel as if I've got nothing left. I'm clinging on, to be honest, and every second that goes by drains even more from me. I think about my bravado in the press conference. I'd felt sure of victory then. Now another, far less welcome, outcome seems inevitable. My stomach turns, my mouth dries. I bite down on my guard and try to stop thinking about defeat.

I'd crippled my body to make weight for the Adonis Stevenson fight. I'd started the camp at fifteen stone six, I needed to get to twelve stone seven. I knew it would be a big ask, but I didn't know how hard it would be. I'd struggled to shed pounds throughout my career and had discovered that losing weight became steadily harder the older I got. There's a photograph of me taken when I was down to thirteen stone three – ten pounds still to lose and there's nothing left of me. I'm a fucking corpse.

I'd felt strong right through camp and then the moment I dipped below 185 pounds, I was fucked, absolutely fucked. I realised then, far too late, that I just couldn't function at any point under thirteen stone three. As I stood on the scales, I thought, *I can't muster anything.* I realised I'd be able to manage two, maybe three minutes of good hard fighting in a thirty-six-minute bout.

That fear was given an extra edge every time I thought about my opponent. He was a vicious hitter: pound for pound, the most dangerous puncher in the world at the time. He was a small fighter, but he had such a long reach. I'd never experienced anything like it.

Stevenson was called Superman. The thing was, he was no hero. There's nothing unusual about a boxer with a past they'd rather not dwell on. But Adonis was fucking nasty. He'd been a violent pimp. He'd beat the prostitutes he controlled or forced them to fight against each other in a gruesome parody of a boxing match, complete with gloves. The women hated him. Two of them had been rendered so desperate by everything he put them through that they actually tried to kill him. When he finally got caught and sent to prison, he'd got into a fight and put another inmate into a coma.

He wasn't the kind of guy you wanted to face when you're drained of all of your power and energy. I knew I'd have to find a way to guide my way through this fight. The problem was, the route didn't seem that clear.

I still had four pounds to lose with an hour before the weigh-in – the only time I'd ever been in that position. The worst of it was that two days before, on the Wednesday, I was bang on the weight. But then I'd eaten two chicken breasts, washed down with 500ml of water, which somehow made me gain five pounds. I got up at 10 a.m. on the morning of the weigh-in, having slept in my tracksuit with the heating on in my room at full blast.

That's how I ended up sitting in a hot bath full of salt. Kerry Kayes, a former bodybuilding champion and the best nutritionist in the world, a guy who'd been with me almost since the beginning, had travelled out to Canada with us.

He said to me, 'Your body is now in a complete state of shock. It won't lose any more weight naturally. You can go on the treadmill for forty minutes and I guarantee you won't lose a single pound. The only way you're going to lose weight now is if you physically draw it out of your body.'

'Great,' I said. 'How can I do that?'

'You have to get in a bath so hot it's going to hurt and it's got to be full of salt.'

We rushed down to the hotel's restaurant, persuaded them to give us a big bag of salt and then sped back up to my room.

Once I'd emptied the salt into the bath, I turned the water on and watched the steam rise as it built up heat. To begin with, I poured ice-cold water on myself. *That hurt,* I thought. Although I soon forget whatever discomfort it had caused. As soon as I stepped into the bath, I felt a pain unlike any I'd ever experienced. There's no agony that compares to feeling your skin burning and knowing that you'll have to endure that experience for another fifteen or twenty minutes.

In a doomed bid to divert my mind, I put Kevin Hart on my iPad and listened to some stand-up. I balanced it precariously on the other end of the bath and during twenty minutes of agony, I alternated between laughing at his jokes and crying at the burning sensation that felt as if it were stripping the skin from every inch of my body. I think it was the closest I've ever come to a mental breakdown. All the while, Fran, who was standing at the foot of the bath, looked on in total shock. My friend Gary, who didn't believe making weight was worth this agony, kept on urging me to get out. But I was already in too far.

It took twenty minutes to force those last four pounds out of my body. For all the good any of this had done me. I hadn't eaten for two days. The last thing that had passed my lips was a single glass of water at 6 p.m. the night before. For almost a week, I'd been draining myself; dragging my energy levels further and further down.

I've never been so convinced that I was dying. One by one, my organs felt like they were shutting down. When you get to that point, it's not just that your tongue is dry and your mouth feels like sandpaper. Although those things were horrible. A moment comes when you can only think about food. Your mind plays tricks. A running tap becomes the source of almost unbearable temptation. You have a paranoid conviction that everybody except you is eating and drinking their fill. It's the kind of mental state that leaves you with scars.

I was fucked.

The weigh-in was nasty, too. All week, Stevenson and his hangers-on had been baiting me, trying to intimidate me. They were just fuckers being cheeky. I wasn't bothered. Instead of dwelling on it, I spent time trying to find out personal information about Stevenson and his team that I could use to my advantage.

When I watch the footage back from the weigh-in, I'm struck by how thin and pale I look, like I need a good meal. Which I did. And then your eyes turn to Stevenson, who was five foot eleven of coiled aggression and strength. He was the kind of fighter who could look dangerous just walking into a room.

When I stared into his eyes as we stood there above the scales and called him a pimp, it was because I wanted to even things up a bit. I saw disbelief on his face and then pure naked rage. It was like he couldn't believe I'd had the nerve to go there. He lost his shit, started getting into my face. I was in my stride by that point, so I started in on his best friend, who followed him around the place like a cheerleader.

'And you can't say anything,' I told him. And then I let him have it using something from his personal life that I knew would mess with his head.

He lost his shit, too. Stevenson came at me and pushed his head in my face. *Fine,* I thought. *If that's the way you want it.* I just pulled my head back and dotted him right on the nose. It might have been the only thing about the fight and the months leading up to it that I actually enjoyed. That was the street in me coming out.

For a few minutes amid all that madness, I felt a sense of exhilaration. I didn't care what happened to Stevenson or whether I'd hurt him. The fracas was over and now the fight was on. I'd made the weight – I was smack bang on twelve stone seven, not an ounce over or under – and I'd seen that I could get to him. I thought, *I'm going to become world champion.* I'd convinced myself that the worst was behind me, so I announced that I'd knock him spark out in three or four rounds. *I'm going to have a good time,* I thought. *This is going to be the one.*

I don't remember much about the fight itself, which is probably for the best, all things considered. All I have is little flashes. Everything else is a blur. There was the brief glimpse I caught of Rachael as I walked to the ring. I hadn't seen her for seven weeks. She had tears in her eyes and it broke my heart in two. I didn't even stop to touch or kiss her. I didn't say anything – I just nodded.

Then there was the sickening understanding that Stevenson possessed an almost supernatural awareness of space. And the dawning realisation that my plan of biding my time and working myself into the fight slowly wasn't working.

The excitement I'd felt at the weigh-in had been replaced by the brutal arithmetic of the situation. I'd dropped so much weight that I knew I couldn't fight for thirty-six minutes. Mick had done a fine job getting me to this point, but now my body had betrayed me. All I had left in me was two minutes of decent work and the conviction that I still had enough to chin him, as long as I got the chance. I'd have to wait for my moment and then knock him out.

But when that moment did come, in the third round,

when I hit him on the side of the head and sent him sprawling on the floor (the referee said he'd slipped – he didn't, I put him down), I couldn't make him pay. That was the end of me. I was on borrowed time after that.

In the sixth round, he caught me with a huge shot that I didn't see coming. There was nothing I could do about it. He hit me so hard I went to sleep on my feet. I went to my corner and bollocked my coach, calling him a fucking idiot because I thought he'd thrown the towel in. He hadn't – it was the referee who'd saved me. In fact, probably saved my life. I was so concussed I had no idea what was going on. The next day, once I could finally bring myself to watch the replay, I had to apologise to him.

Defeat is the loneliest place in the world. You feel as if you've got no one, that you're on your own. I never classed Nathan Cleverly as having beaten me. After that fight, I wasn't really scarred, I thought I'd won. I was more annoyed than anything. In my head I'd been the better fighter on the night. As I saw it, Stevenson was the first genuine loss of my career. I'd given everything and it wasn't enough, which broke my heart. I knew that I had to work to recreate myself and get back into the mix. But knowing that was easy. Doing that was hard.

Once everything was over, I went back to my hotel room. I didn't want to speak to anyone. I didn't see my wife. Nobody. The idea of other people seeing or talking to me seemed impossible. I feared it'd crush whatever was left in me. I lay there in my room and cried myself to sleep. Maybe other things happened, maybe not. I don't remember much from that night.

When I woke the next day, the embarrassment and shame began all over again: you don't want to be seen, so you just try to disappear. As you move around the hotel, you keep your cap on and your head down – you don't want to speak to anyone.

After all the big-up and all the build-up, after all the talk of 'I'm going to do this, I'm going to do that, I'm going to be a world champion,' I'd been stopped on my feet. I was out cold standing up. I never believed that could happen to me. And yet it had. As far as I was concerned, nothing I'd achieved mattered any more. I was a failure.

When you've had a setback, everything can feel like it's falling apart at the seams. It can feel like the world is against you and that you've lost control. Everything is fucked, your dreams are dead and you're never going to get to where you want to go. One of the best things I did after the Adonis Stevenson fight was to start taking positive steps almost immediately.

In the empty days that followed my defeat, I spent a lot of time thinking. That kind of setback makes you question yourself. I went over what had happened again and again. A couple of things were immediately clear: the buck stopped with me. It was nobody else's fault. I was the fighter. It was me who got into the ring. I was the one who'd trained for months on end. I was the one who'd been beaten.

I had to work out where I'd gone wrong. What weaknesses in me or my preparation had the fight exposed? It was a process that demanded complete honesty. Watching the fight back, it was immediately obvious to me that I'd left it too late to go for Stevenson. That had been a massive mistake.

It hadn't just been a question of poor tactics. As broken as I felt, there was still enough of me that believed I was good enough to be a world champion. But I knew I couldn't carry on doing old things the old way and hoping for a new result. I was fooling myself if I thought that fighting at light heavyweight was making the most of my abilities. I wasn't really throwing punches against Stevenson, I was waving my hands at him. It was exciting to think that once I started fighting at my proper weight division, I was going to be so much more powerful and dangerous. At cruiserweight, my punch would regain the ferocity that I'd always been so proud of.

That was the first positive step I could take. I started lifting weights within four days of the fight. You could see the difference almost immediately, as I began to look far bigger and healthier. I was taking on proper nutrition, powerlifting and thriving on the idea that my training would now be about improving as a fighter rather than running endless miles to try to make 175 pounds.

As good as it felt to be back in the gym like this, I also

knew that I was putting off something that I had to do, even if the thought of it alone was killing me. Right through the whole camp I'd had a nagging feeling that something was wrong. That feeling had only grown once we'd reached Canada. But it was only as I sat miserable on the flight home that I could really admit it to myself. I needed a new coach and I needed to find a new way of preparing for fights.

Mick McAllister had been a brilliant coach for me for years. He knew me and my game inside out. In fact, it was Mick who'd been on at me for a long time to go to cruiserweight, because he always thought I'd be better at that level. More than that, he was a huge part of my life. He was one of those men who gave so much passion and energy to the Rotunda without ever asking for a penny in return. It was never about the money with Mick. He'd put years into my career, from the very earliest days, through to the ABA titles and beyond. He'd been there right through, sacrificing time with family and friends in order to help me.

And yet he was sixty years old. I couldn't expect him to be able to do the things physically that he'd been able to pull off a decade before. He was also old-fashioned about quite a lot of things, too. Mick had always been an absolutely amazing amateur coach, but deep down, I didn't believe that he'd be able to give me what I needed to go to the next level of the professional game. I needed new perspectives. I needed someone who could challenge me in fresh ways.

In addition to that, I'd started to think that the way we

were doing camps was wrong. During our preparations for the Adonis Stevenson fight, we'd followed a familiar path. The first section was in Liverpool. I'd be back and forth between the Rotunda and my home, somehow trying to squeeze in what I thought was a normal family life alongside it.

I'd wake up at home and my kids would see me get out of bed, but very soon I'd be in my training gear off to the gym. When I returned, I'd be empty and tired. Whenever the boys tried to speak to me, I'd tell them that I was tired and that they needed to leave me alone. I didn't want to speak – I just wanted to eat my food and then go to bed. This would go on for three months. I was physically present and yet mentally, I was barely there at all. All the same, it was an existence I'd got used to and I couldn't really imagine any other. I was like a fish: I almost didn't realise there was a world outside water.

After that, I lived with McAllister, Fran and Gary in Jersey City for four weeks before we went on to Quebec for the fight. We'd followed that routine two or three times before. The others enjoyed being there and were desperate to help in any way they could, but I realised that wasn't an environment that was right for me. It was good having mates around you on rest days, when we could go on walks or to shopping centres or wherever the fuck. The rest of the time, however, I realised I needed to be on my own so I could focus on the fight. When I'm by myself, then I'm not worried about whether other people are bored or happy. I can give my full attention to the stuff I know is most important at that moment in time. I don't expect anything and nobody expects anything from me. I needed to be lonely when I was in camp to get the best out of myself. That might sound selfish, but it's what I realised I needed.

Dave Coldwell was the obvious person for me to speak to. Dave had so much experience and expertise. He'd learned an incredible amount from working with the great Brendan Ingle and had then gone on to train some of the best fighters around. He was also very definitely based in Sheffield, where his family lived. It's possible that if I'd offered him head-spinning money, he might have dragged his roots up and hauled them over to Merseyside, but him being on the wrong side of the Pennines was what I wanted. There was one other thing. Although Dave had trained world champions before, he'd never made one. I thought the idea that I could be his first would be another incentive – for both of us.

When I called Dave about potentially taking a role, he'd actually taken a step back from training. But he didn't need much persuasion. Mick would be another matter.

To begin with, I tried for a compromise. I took Mick to Long Lane boxing club and I said, 'Mick, we need help. We need to bring someone in. And I think the person we should bring in is Dave Coldwell.'

'What do you mean?' he asked.

'I just think now we're going to move to cruiserweight, he's the ideal person to bring in.'

'No,' he said, 'I'm not answering to no one. I'm the coach.'

'You're going to be the coach. You're going to be in the corner. But bringing him in will be a great addition to me going to cruiserweight and also he can do the physical work.'

'No, absolutely not, no.'

That left me with a tough decision. I knew Dave was the key to me making a success of going to cruiserweight. I had no doubt about that. But there was still a part of me that was saying, 'It's safer to keep things the same. You're comfortable where you are now. Why risk ripping everything up and starting again in a city you barely know?' On top of all this, I knew that Mick would take it hard if I left. I didn't want to leave him, because I felt such a strong sense of gratitude to him for everything he'd done. I had so much love and respect for him; in many ways, he was like a grandfather to me.

I went with Dave. Mick hasn't spoken to me since. We were fifteen years in – he'd coached me ever since I was a kid at the Rotunda. I can understand his hurt, but I hope he knows how much I still adore him. I'll always think the world of Mick and I'll always love his wife, Julie, and his children, Mick and Hayley. I'm so grateful for everything he did for me and although I wish we still had a relationship, I've got to accept that he's made his choice.

As far as I'm concerned, the decision I took had nothing to do with Mick's abilities. It was all about me and what I needed for my family. If I saw the chance to learn something new from another trainer, then I had to take it. A fighter only gets one career, so sometimes they have to do things that can appear selfish. We're not like coaches, who get to work with dozens of boxers. And ultimately, I was the one taking punches. I was the one who was going out there and getting hurt.

I hated having to make that call and yet I knew deep down it was the right thing to do. I wouldn't have become world champion if it hadn't been for Dave Coldwell. In a game in which any fool can claim to be a boxing coach as long as they've paid the fee to get the licence, Dave stands out as a proper teacher. He educates fighters, providing them with skills and techniques they didn't even know they needed. Along with Jimmy Albertina, he's the best thing that ever happened to my career.

It was clear from the very first day that Dave and I were going to work well together, even if his methods and techniques were different to anything I'd experienced before and were at times hard to get my head around. It wasn't so much that he was a better coach than Mick had been. It was more that he offered a completely different approach, which was exactly what I needed at that point in my career.

I started learning new things the second I walked into his gym. Dave added layers to my game. Mick McAllister had been obsessively focused on my feet, which meant that my footwork was brilliant. Dave recognised what I was good at and he wasn't interested in messing about with stuff that didn't need to be fixed. But he was also able to understand where I had room to improve, like my defence and my counter-punching, and then he worked relentlessly to force me to become better.

Dave worked me hard. He didn't just have a deep under-standing of my strengths and weaknesses, he also knew how to get the best out of me. He was quicker to praise me than Jimmy had been. At the same time, he was always on at me, challenging me to push myself even harder. He'd say things like, 'How much do you really want it? I always hear you say no one will ever want it more than you, but how much do you *really* want it?' That would always light a fire under my arse. Sometimes we'd clash over something he'd asked me to do and we'd end up not speaking to each other for days. Other times I'd get a cob on but work even harder, just to prove him wrong.

He was just like Jimmy Albertina in that respect: all I ever wanted to do was impress him. And you couldn't buy his respect, you had to earn it. So when he had a little dig at me, my reaction would be: 'I'll show you how much I fucking want it, you twat.' Then I'd go and do extra work in the gym. Sometimes I'd stay in the gym an extra half an hour just to annoy him.

Although my training was going well – I'd easily put on the two stone extra I needed to fight as a cruiserweight – I couldn't ever quite shake off the anxieties that had accumulated after my loss at Stevenson's hands. Defeat hadn't just been a massive blow to my pride, it had also affected my confidence.

I'd never questioned my chin before and yet, as my first fight back approached, I found myself asking: 'Can I still take a shot?' Dave had done so much to rebuild my confidence after my defeat, but when it was time for sparring, Dave had brought in a relatively unknown cruiserweight who turned out to be a bit of a puncher. I was levels above this guy and yet I found myself thinking, *just keep away from me – I don't need to get clocked early.*

I realised that I'd felt the impact of getting stopped by Stevenson much more deeply than I'd first thought. It was sending my mind haywire. I was second-guessing myself, trying to work out how worried and afraid I really was. It was hard to convince myself that I truly was a contender.

And then Eddie Hearn, who I think had lost a bit of faith in me ever becoming world champion, matched me with a bruiser called Valery Brudov, who'd more knockout wins under his belt than I'd had fights. When you come up to a new weight division, you're supposed to be matched up with a nice easy touch – Brudov was anything but.

Right from the earliest seconds, it was clear he was dangerous. He rocked me straight away. He caught me on the top of the head and for a couple of seconds, everything just went. It wasn't enough to knock me down, but that clip was enough to let me know that he was there and that I was in a fight. From that moment on, I was very wary . . . right up until the final round, when I knocked him unconscious with a left hook that threw him flat on his back so hard and so fast that he snapped his ankle in half on the way down.

Even after that victory, the memory of what happened against Adonis Stevenson stayed with me. I was heartbroken and the defeat haunted me for the next five or six fights. It was always on my mind. I was desperate for revenge, but whatever Stevenson said, I knew there was no chance that he'd have fought me at cruiserweight, because we both knew I'd have eaten him alive. It wasn't until I beat Nathan Cleverly in our rematch that I was able to rid myself of the memory. Smashing the great cardio machine to pieces over twelve rounds, outboxing and outworking him every step of the way, helped me to put it all to bed.

After that, I could get on with my career.

IF YOU WORK HARD, YOU CAN TRANSFORM FAILURE INTO OPPORTUNITY

Defeats or failures are always the end of something. This means that if you look at them in a different way, they can also represent the beginning of something new. I could have looked at that loss and decided the only thing I needed to change was to fight in the right weight class. I could have blamed everything on that. But I learned really important things after I was beaten by Adonis Stevenson. One of them was the freedom to start again. Without that loss, I don't think I'd have made all the changes that ultimately led to me winning the world title. If I hadn't been beaten that night in Quebec, if I hadn't had that bleak period of soul-searching, I wouldn't have hired Dave Coldwell, I wouldn't have moved to Sheffield, I wouldn't have achieved all of my dreams at Goodison Park.

When things are ticking on, when they're OK, it can be dangerous. You get used to thinking that because something is good enough, then there's no need to change it. It gets to the point when the idea of mixing things up can start to feel like it's not worth the effort or you get frightened of doing what, deep down, you probably know needs to be done. To begin with, that defeat felt like it was the end of everything. Instead, it was actually the jolt I needed.

THAT'S ON ME

When people suffer a setback, they tend to do one of two things. They'll either double down and say, 'Actually, I was doing the right thing before, I just got unlucky. I'll carry on doing the same thing again and again.' Or they can be humble and accept that they need to make changes.

Very few boxers ever shoulder the blame; they're cowards, the lot of them. It's a habit that starts when they're young: amateur fighters lose a fight and then move to another gym because they convince themselves that it was the coach's fault.

And that mentality persists right through the career of ninety per cent of fighters. They'll claim they weren't trained right, or they weren't given the right advice or nutrition or whatever the fuck. My view is always, 'Well listen, mate, you knew that before the fucking fight.'

The stuff that Deontay Wilder came out with after he was beaten by Tyson Fury was crazy. He doesn't genuinely believe that Tyson Fury's gloves were fiddled with. He doesn't genuinely believe that Tyson Fury punched him with the wrist part of his glove. That's insane. He *knows* that's insane. But he's got that many yes-men around him telling him what they think he wants to hear that he's actually ended up buying into the hype and the nonsense.

What he should have done instead was sit down and think properly about what really happened and why. It's very hard to be very honest with yourself, because sometimes you're not going to like what you uncover. It's always going to be easier to blame other people. But if you want to get the right results, in any walk of life, you've got to face up to the reality of the situation you're in. When you look in the mirror, you'll know deep down where it went wrong. There's only so many times you can tell yourself the same bullshit before you admit to yourself that, 'Yes, that was my fault. That's on me.'

You have to be brutal. Don't tell yourself comforting fairy tales about why you failed. That's not going to help anyone. Look at it as a sort of audit. Go through what *actually* happened and *why* with the attitude of a forensic accountant.

How did it start? How did it end? When were the mistakes actually made? Defeat is the best teacher. You learn more lessons when you lose than you ever do when you win. Lessons are always there, you just have to be willing to look for them.

That's the process I put myself through after the Stevenson fight. I knew that my approach to making weight had been wrong. I also recognised that I'd chosen to ignore certain things that I knew should have been fixed because I was hoping against hope that they'd resolve themselves on their own. Which, clearly, they didn't. It was fucking difficult. It was also upsetting enough that at one point, I began to cry, but it was also absolutely essential. The end result of me doing that was that I began to put the building blocks in place that would eventually become the foundation of my later success.

Everyone knows how crushing failures or defeats can feel – whatever the circumstances. What you have to try to do is recognise them as a chance to begin again.

DON'T THROW THE BABY OUT WITH THE BATHWATER

You have to be uncompromising in your search for what went wrong, but don't lose sight of the things that went well, no matter how tempting it might be to want to make a completely fresh start. Dave Coldwell recognised this. He was brilliant at introducing me to new techniques and yet he never tried to interfere with the parts of my game that had taken me to this point. I knew my footwork – my ability to dance while other people my weight only stepped – was a valuable asset, so it would have been foolish to try to reinvent it after one loss. So many boys go from amateur boxing to the professional ranks and forget their footwork along the way, which just turns them into mummies. They end up forgetting about body shots entirely and go 'headhunting' through every fight. I was never interested in limiting myself like that. At the end of the day, it's far better to add to your arsenal of skills than it is to subtract from them.

The other mistake you should be wary of making is over-interpreting a bad day. Sometimes you'll fail to perform not because you've prepared poorly or don't have the necessary skills, but because you woke that morning not feeling 100 per cent or you're distracted by problems elsewhere in your life. Be sure that the change you think you need to implement is necessary. Remember: even legends lose.

GET BACK ON THE HORSE

Whatever setback you've experienced, you have to accept that it's done, it's over. You can't sit there hoping that the result will be overturned or that some act of God will make everything OK again. Because if you're still holding on to that false hope, you won't be doing the important work of starting again. It's so important that you generate momentum as soon as you can. The longer you leave it, the harder it'll get. If I'd sat around and moped for a few months after the Stevenson loss, I know for a fact that I'd have ended up totally fixated on all the things I couldn't do, rather than reminding myself how good I was and how far I still had to go. That's why I was back in the gym within a week of my loss in Quebec. That's why I was so keen to fight again as quickly as possible.

If you've lost out on getting a job, then instead of dwelling on it or feeling sorry for yourself, get back out there and carry on with your search. It feels good to seize the initiative. My defeats made me a better fighter because they showed me what I could do better. Don't treat a knockback as something closing down. It's just given you the answer to solve the next situation. Before long, you'll find that disappointment is replaced by hope.

231

SUMMARY

- Failure is a fact of life. You can't avoid it, so why not try to transform the ruins of your present into the foundations of your future?

- Don't spare yourself in the aftermath of a setback. Find out what went wrong and why. Then commit to doing better next time. Never try to spread responsibility around by blaming others.

- Never forget what got you to this point. Just because you've failed once, it doesn't mean that you're a failure. And you shouldn't jettison everything that made you successful in the first place. Use failure as an opportunity to add to your arsenal, not subtract from it.

- Try to move on as soon as you can. If you spend too much time dwelling on your failure, you'll end up stuck in your past when you could be building your future.

CHAPTER 9
BIG MOUTH STRIKES AGAIN

BJ Flores thinks you can say what you want and avoid the consequences. BJ Flores thinks the stuff we've said to each other is just trash talk. BJ Flores is a fucking idiot.

I'm different. I might have said stuff for effect before, but this time I mean every word. When I say I'm going to murder him, it's not braggadocio, it's the cold, hard, brutal truth.

He's made this chance for himself by stalking me. Fair play. And he's talked shit every time we've come face to face. What he needs to understand is that every time I go into the ring, I'm fighting for my life. It's not a game for me. It's not bright lights and glory; I know there's nothing glamorous about getting your hands, nose or ribs smashed. And yet, if I have to get off the floor a hundred times, I will. I'm dirty, I'm vicious, I don't care how I win.

Flores is an Instagram fighter. He exists to throw tough poses in front of the camera. Whereas I've come out to hurt him. I know I look like the sort of traveller who scraps in car parks. Fuck. I don't care. When I hit somebody when I'm wearing ten-ounce gloves, they're going to feel it. You might think I don't really come across

233

like a professional athlete. You might think I'm a bit chunky, a bit flabby. But when I hit you for the first time, you're going to think: What. Was. That?

In the first seconds of the fight, Flores still seems confident. It's as if he hasn't listened to a single word of all the warnings I've given him over the last couple of weeks. He still doesn't realise that I was being serious. And for the first couple of rounds, he even holds his own. But by the third round I can see fear in his eyes. He's fought a lot of big punchers, but nobody has ever damaged him like this. Nobody has ever blitzed and bamboozled him.

The last few minutes have taught him two big lessons. Number one: I'm the best cruiserweight in the world. Number two: words mean something. If you want to run your mouth off, that's fine, that's the risk you've chosen to take. But you'd better be very fucking ready to back up everything you say.

The only fight in my whole career that I went into with an agenda was my first defence of the WBC title, against BJ Flores. Except, I wasn't thinking about him – he was just a stepping stone. My focus was almost entirely on David Haye.

Everything had shifted after I'd beaten Makabu. I'd become world champion, the thing I'd dreamed of for so long, and yet here I was, in my shitty hotel room, still doing the same thing as I had when I was a challenger. At night I started thinking: *I've done all the stuff I was supposed to do, why hasn't my life really changed? What am I doing this for? Why am I in Sheffield? Why am I putting my wife and kids through this?*

Why am I putting myself through this? Why can't I force Dave Coldwell to move to Liverpool?

It would go over and over and over in my head. I'd achieved all of my goals and dreams. In that respect, I didn't need to fight any more. But we were far from set up and my pride alone couldn't support my family. Fighting could. And if wanted to secure our financial future, a bout with David Haye, one of British boxing's biggest draw at the time, was the obvious answer.

I didn't particularly want to fight Flores. I thought he was a tit then. In fact, I still do now. He's just a pretty boy from Miami who jumps on everybody else's ship and who thinks he's Johnny Big Bollocks. He'd been following me everywhere for what felt like years. Like an absolute knob, he'd turned up at the *Creed* premiere in London with David Haye and was busy chatting shit about how I was just a blown-up light heavyweight. He reckoned I'd never do anything at cruiserweight, could never beat him. Which I thought was an interesting opinion.

It was the fact that he was David Haye's best mate that caught my eye. Eddie had been on at me to fight Flores for a while. I said I would, but only if he could guarantee that Haye would be on ringside commentary. Eddie didn't really understand why I was so keen and I kept my thoughts to myself. But off he went and set it up.

Right through the camp, all the training with Dave Coldwell had been really good, yet I could tell that my mindset wasn't quite right. Usually I'd be spending fight week desperately trying to stop myself from obsessing about the man I was about to go toe-to-toe with. This time round, I realised I was struggling even to focus on Flores. All I could see was David Haye. Which, when I look back on it, was unbelievably stupid of me. Actually, it was worse – it was dangerous.

Nobody had ever knocked BJ Flores out. He'd been in with three world champions previously and had only lost the last one in a split decision, which a lot of people thought should have been given to him. And he had all the motivation in the world: he was that close to achieving his dream in the champion's backyard. But that didn't interest me. When the thought crossed my mind of the fight that was actually coming up, I just said to myself: 'I'm the world champion. I'm going to blast you out in a couple of rounds.' I crashed the weight, picked up an injury to my left hand in my final sparring session and ignored all of it.

I looked shit on the scales when we weighed in, but then so did he. I knew he'd done the weight wrong, trying to shed too many pounds at the last minute, which I knew would leave his body more vulnerable than it would have otherwise. I carried on feeling upbeat. Not quite carefree and yet not too far off it, either. It was only later that night that I suddenly realised that I couldn't afford to lose the fight, because the shame of being defeated on my first defence would be too much. I hated the idea of being remembered as somebody who'd won a title, then spewed it almost straight away, like Tony Tucker, whose reign as world champion lasted a mere sixty-four days.

Even when I got into the ring, even when BJ Flores started eyeballing me, I was only looking at David Haye. Right through the fight, it was David Haye's voice I heard over all the noise in the arena, shouting instructions to his friend from the seat he'd taken in the neutral corner. When BJ Flores looked at me, he saw a championship belt. Whereas I was looking at that tit sitting outside the ring, about to watch his friend get battered, and I saw financial security for my family. David Haye held the keys to my kingdom. It was a calculated risk that I was willing to back up. I knew exactly what I was doing. I went about my business and I made it count.

I turned to David Haye: 'I'm going to fuck you. I'm going to fucking do you in.' All the while, he was sitting there shaking his head in disbelief. It felt like a good idea at the time. I look back now on how I behaved and think, *you absolute tit.* Now that I've got to know him properly, I regret a lot of my behaviour towards Haye – I've changed my opinion of him, he's a sound guy – and yet at the time, all I wanted was to wind him up.

I thought I was levels above Flores. I didn't care about him at all. Before the sound of the first bell had died away, I started taking risks I should never even have been contemplating. I was quicker, stronger and more efficient. I should have been aiming to break him down slowly and yet I got drawn into just trading punches. It was as if I'd forgotten my jab completely. I copped him with a left hook and then he got me with a left hand on the chin. Either of us could have got knocked out. All it needed was for him to catch me on the chin bang on just once and I'd have gone down. I was lucky that the work I'd done with David Coldwell could get me through that fight.

It was a contest in which skill and strategy were less important than aggression and resilience. We were in a brawl and there was no point pretending otherwise. At one point I twatted him one, aimed at the body, but it went so low that I caught him right in the bollocks. It was that kind of fight. He stepped back full of outrage, appealing to the referee, who because he'd been blindsided, hadn't seen anything wrong and just told him to get on with it. Flores was so busy moaning at the referee that he forgot the first rule of boxing: defend yourself at all times. He should have kept his hands up; he didn't and I took advantage of that. Fuck off, I smacked him with another left hook to his chin and boom, he went down.

Almost before Flores had crashed down onto the canvas, I'd walked over to David Haye: 'You're next. You're fucking getting it.' That's why I'd taken those risks: because I wanted him to see me demolish Flores right before his eyes.

I dropped Flores three more times after that. The last time was the only punch in the whole fight that I'd caught him as cleanly as I wanted, but it was enough. Within seconds I was over to Haye again, screaming and spitting through my gumshield. Something happened then. There

238

was a feral chaotic energy in that crowd. It was like they'd smelled blood. And I kicked the inflatable Toblerone that was balanced on the edge of the ring and it had arrowed into his face. 'Fight me. Fight me.' That's when I leaped over the ropes and went for Haye.

I'm not thick. I wasn't going to start a fight while I was wearing boxing gloves and bandaged hands when he'd be there with his bare fists. As if. There was part of me that wanted to give him a belt if I could get close enough, but part of me knew that it would be a very stupid thing to do. I knew damn well that the security guards would get to me before I was anywhere near him. Thank fuck they did.

Red-faced, glistening with sweat, I carried on screaming at Haye, my scratched voice carrying over the roars and shrieks of the crowd. I was hurling threats at him even when I disappeared underneath a mountain of security guys. Haye just stood there, immaculate in his grey suit. For a while he had a complacent smile plastered all over his face, as if he were amused by what he'd seen. But if you watch the footage closely in the minutes that followed, you could see something else beneath his grin: he was rattled.

The whole world could see that I'd laid down a challenge. And now the whole world wanted to see David Haye smash this cocky Scouser prick to bits. He'd gone into that arena to commentate on a fight and he'd come away knowing he'd have to go toe-to-toe with a maniac. Except, of course, that all that craziness had been for show. And I think Haye knew that, which is why he was so unsettled by what he'd witnessed.

It was a weird night. I'd just stopped a man who'd never been stopped, not even by three other world champions. I smashed him inside three rounds. It might have been an ugly fight – one of the worst, and certainly the riskiest, of my career – but it was also a standout result. And yet *nobody*, least of all me, had the slightest bit of interest in that. The 9,000 fans who walked out of the Echo Arena that night didn't waste a word on BJ Flores or my performance. All they were saying was: 'Did you see Bellew attack Haye?'

YOU MAKE YOUR OWN LUCK

I've got two things going for me: I've always been able to punch like fuck and I'll tell anybody that they're a gobshite. I started out flattening journeymen who couldn't knock the skin off a rice pudding. And as soon as the fight was over, I'd head to the nearest camera and announce that, 'I will fucking baptise anyone.' Those words mattered; they made sure I was on television for my next fight. They forced people to talk about me.

You can't let people be indifferent towards you. Whether they love you or hate you, make them think about you. I understood that from the get-go and as a result, I was a promoter's dream. I always sold the whole show. There are fighters out there who could be megastars: all they need to do is open their mouths. I talk. Sometimes I've ended up making a tit of myself, which is why more than one person has tried to encourage me to curb what I say and let the boxing do the talking. Most of the time, however, it's worked out.

I did all that because I knew, even then, that if you want to move forwards, sometimes you have to give fate a helpful little push. In boxing, there's no such thing as a fluky punch. It doesn't matter if your eyes are closed. If you throw that left hook and it lands, it was *meant* to land. I was always on my toes, looking for new opportunities, because I knew that I couldn't afford to sit around waiting for them to come my way. I used Twitter to make my first world title fight: Nathan Cleverly's opponent Jürgen Brähmer had pulled out, so I created an account and announced that I'd fight him. And that's why I made sure David Haye was ringside commentator for the BJ Flores fight: I wanted Sky cameras to catch me calling him a pussy, because I knew that he'd have to fight me next. The boxing public loves a good rivalry.

I know that a lot of the time it can feel easier to glide through life on autopilot, taking things as they come, but I guarantee that after a while, you'll start to feel frustrated. You'll begin to wonder why it's other people who get what look to you like lucky opportunities. You'll ask yourself why it is that although you feel as if you're working hard all the time, you're not making the kind of progress you'd envisaged. You'll begin to think: *maybe I should have taken a few more risks.*

BE YOUR OWN CHEERLEADER

Maybe more than any other sport, in boxing you have to open your mouth and sell yourself. If you don't understand that, you won't make it.

I learned about the power of self-promotion at an early age. It was another of the things that came from studying fighters. I looked at the likes of Hector Camacho, Fernando Vargas, Prince Naseem Hamed, James Toney and Roy Jones Jr. and paid attention to how they sold themselves, how they presented themselves to the people who were paying to watch them. As I watched, I tried to take little parts from each of them that I could use for myself.

Mike Tyson didn't say much and when he did, it was something nasty. With him it was very much a case of his actions speaking louder than his words. If you're the sort of person who does the majority of his communication by smashing other boxers' faces in, people will want to see you.

Hector Camacho knocked guys out too, but what really sold him was his braggadocio. To be honest, he couldn't burst an egg, and yet he still found a way of intimidating people. He'd insult you, wear obnoxious clothes, anything to get a rise. Ricardo Mayorga used to smoke cigars and eat pizzas while he stood on the scales during the weigh-in.

Nigel Benn played on his reputation for being vicious and mean and it worked for him. Whereas Chris Eubank dressed himself up in tweeds and ran around lisping 'Hello, sir.' They were all amazing boxers. At the same time, they were amazing showmen. Because they knew that professional boxing is also professional showbusiness. That was where all the feuds and rivalries came from.

Good, I thought, *I'll emulate that.*

Everyone in Liverpool is always striving and fighting. It's the only place in the world I know where everyone has the mentality of 'I've got to get on,' which is why it was surprising that as I was coming up as a boxer, there was nobody really flying the flag for the city, nobody really lighting up the game.

Lots of fighters had loads of ability, but none of them really knew how to talk the talk. People like Joe McNally were brilliant in the ring and yet they weren't interested in all the stuff that went on outside. Ultimately, that hurt him. I tried my best for Joe, putting him forwards for Hayemaker and then Frank Warren, but it never happened for him. He had a handful of bouts but if he'd been given the opportunity I still believe he could have been a European champion. All he needed was that one big match that would have showed everybody how good he was. Which is a shame – he would have pissed the British championships. Instead, he lost out to the shitty, political side of the game.

That's not the same as saying he and others like him had bad luck. They just didn't want to do the talking. It didn't matter that they were better boxers than me – I was a better promoter than them. No other amateur was saying or doing the things I was. I was the only fighter who understood what needed to be done and I was the only one who understood that I'd have to accept hate as well as love if I wanted to make it.

It's a sad but true fact that the people who get ahead are those who make others sit up and pay attention. If you don't tell people how hard you're working or what sort of a difference you've made, there's no guarantee that anybody else will notice. If you've done something well at work, celebrate it. Otherwise you might find yourself being passed over in favour of other louder-mouthed colleagues.

SET YOUR OWN PACE

When I went to the Rotunda that first time and Jimmy told me I wasn't going to box for at least eighteen months, I thought, *fuck this, I'm ready to box now.* I wanted to get out there and test myself in a proper fight, because I knew that doing so would massively accelerate my development. I might have had my tail between my legs ahead of my return to Jimmy's gym almost two years later, but I was also already on my way up. They knew who I was now, they'd seen me render people unconscious, so I wasn't some scraggly kid who'd turned up on their door. I had a record and a medical card with my bouts on it.

Be honest with yourself. If you've still got work to do or things that you need to improve, then cool your jets for a bit. But if you truly do believe you're ready, then don't let other people hold you back. The last thing you want to do is stagnate when you could be greedily hoovering up new experiences and skills.

TAKE CALCULATED RISKS

So much of boxing is about assessing the ratio of risk and reward. Just getting into the ring against a man who's determined to smash your face in is a risk. At the beginning of your career, when you're fighting journeymen, you don't think so much about losing. It's only when you progress through the ranks and start facing world-class fighters that risk really comes into the equation.

That's when you realise that the odds are no longer stacked in your favour. The 90/10 walkovers become 50/50 battles. You have to start asking yourself whether you really think you can win. You have to assess how many things he can do better than you. How much experience or size or weight am I giving away to him?

When I faced Isaac Chilemba, I knew he'd catch me a lot. I reckoned I'd have to be willing to take four punches clean in the face for every six I landed on him. My bet was that I'd be able to absorb everything he had and then outwork him. It was a calculated gamble, which I wouldn't have made with any other fighter. If I'd tried that approach with David Haye, I'd have been knocked out in the first round.

But it's at that elite level that the rewards can be out of this world. I took a risk by fighting Ilunga Makabu when nobody else would. I fought David Haye even after he threatened to put me into a coma. The risks were evident and yet so were the rewards. That fight not only made me more money than I'd ever even seen in my life, but my victory also elevated me to the top rank of box office fighters.

At some point, if you want to achieve your dreams, you'll have to take risks. That might be remortgaging your home in order to finance a business or swapping a comfortable salary for an uncertain self-employed future.

I threw myself into the BJ Flores fight without really taking my opponent seriously because I was absolutely set on forcing David Haye to take me on. That was a risk and yet I was willing to accept it, because the potential benefits were, for me, worth it. And it was a calculated risk, because although I didn't prepare for Flores as diligently as I might another opponent, I also knew that my performance levels had skyrocketed since becoming world champion. I was fighting out of my skin.

When you're considering doing something that takes you out of your comfort zone, you've got to be upfront about what you stand to lose and what you stand to gain. You also have to have a clear sense of your abilities. I'm not here to say everyone can will themselves into becoming a world champion.

Ultimately, everyone has a very different stomach for risk. I can't tell you how much uncertainty you should expose yourself to – that has to be a personal decision – but I will tell you this: you cannot eliminate all risk from your life. In fact, if you want to get anywhere, at some point you're going to have to embrace it.

THE HARDER YOU WORK, THE LUCKIER YOU GET

It's no good putting yourself in good positions if you're not in the right mindset to take advantage when you get there. As soon as you get that opening, make sure you commit to it 100 per cent. Try to maximise the chances of converting that opportunity into an achievement.

Ultimately, it all has to be backed up with hard work. You can't wing your way through life, no matter how charming or clever you think you are. If you've made promises, make sure you keep them. If you say you're going to be somewhere, make sure you're there. Don't let carelessness be the thing that undermines all the great work you've done.

I was obsessive about getting everything right before I fought. I wanted to square every element away so that I could be confident that I was giving myself the absolute best chance of victory. I knew that I'd created an amazing opportunity for myself by getting to that point, so I couldn't let anything undermine it.

No detail was too small, because those tiny margins

could have been the difference between success and failure. They're the first things that can slip your mind, but very often they'll be the first things to slip you up. That's why I'd turn up at a venue three hours before I actually needed to: I wanted to make sure that whatever happened – traffic, mistakes, cock-ups – I was still going to be there on time. And it would have been no good going into a bout in incredible shape if I was lazy about my kit. So I'd get my hands wrapped a good hour before the action, because there had been times early in my career when my hands felt great for the first five minutes after they'd been wrapped and then I realised they'd gone numb because the blood had stopped. If I'd left that kind of thing to the last minute and hadn't given myself time to fix mistakes, it could have been fatal.

I even took responsibility for the way my low blow was fitted. I'd personally wind the duct tape around my waistband. Then I'd put the low blow on. Only when I was confident it was safe and secure would I then add another layer of duct tape. I'd wrap it round my body once to tighten it, then twist it so the sticky side was facing out before taking it round my body for another layer. Then, when I put my shorts on, they'd stick to the low blow. There was no way they'd move even a millimetre during the whole fight. (This was great for the bout itself, not so great for the moment fifteen minutes before it begins when I remember I need a shit and have try to wipe my arse while wearing my boxing gloves.)

One thing I've found is that coming from where I do,

people tend to make generalisations about me. They're not always favourable. There's not much I can do to change their prejudices, but I can work hard to try to give them as few opportunities as possible to dismiss me out of hand.

So, when I was outside the whole circus of fights and weigh-ins and all that bullshit, I'd be unfailingly polite and respectful. I'll always make sure I say please and thank you. I'll hold the door open for anyone, no matter how old they are. (Obviously, if somebody crosses me, then I chuck those manners out of the window. I'm a polite but very fucking angry driver. I'll wave, let you go, stuff like that, but the minute you've done me, I'll lose my fucking shit straight away.)

Presenting yourself properly is important. In my opinion, everything from your shoes up represents who you are. I can't bear it when somebody turns up wearing rotten trainers. I can't have it. If I walk into a consultation with somebody who I'm meeting for the first time and they're not appropriately dressed, I'm tempted to leave straight away: if they're not taking it seriously, what's the point in being there? I might know fuck-all about what we're discussing, I might not be the brightest there, but I tell you what, I'll look the part.

Recently, I realised that my trainers had dirt on them, so I went into JD Sports, bought another pair and put them straight on. Nobody has any excuse not to be clean and smart. Have a shower, make sure you smell nice. Do that, be on time – *always* be on time – show that you've prepared and you'll gain respect.

FUCK 'EM

People will tell you you're not good enough. People will tell you that it's not your turn or you don't deserve it. People will tell you it's not your time. People will say that you're not strong or fast enough. People will tell you that you don't want it enough. People will tell you that you're doing it for the wrong reasons. People will tell you that you're aiming too high. People will tell you that the odds are stacked against you. People will tell you a lot of shite. Ignore them.

When people flood you with negativity, there's only one response: fuck 'em. Whenever anybody told me I couldn't do anything, I used what they said as motivation. Always be open to positive criticism, but you should bat everything else away. If they don't like what you're doing, that's their problem, not yours.

SUMMARY

- Nobody is going to hand you opportunities. Make them for yourself. You only score from the shots you take and good fortune is only ever half the story.

- Don't be afraid of opening your mouth and celebrating your achievements. If *you* don't do that, who else will do it for you?

- Only you will know when you're ready to take the next step, so don't wait for the invitation. If you're happy that you really are in a position to push on, then don't hesitate. Work to your timetable, not other people's.

- When you've made that chance for yourself, make sure you're in the best possible place to seize it. Don't let that opportunity slip away because you haven't prepared properly.

CHAPTER 10

NO MATTER WHAT YOU HIT ME WITH, YOU CANNOT HURT ME

Haye has me backed against the corner. It's the third round of our first match against each other. When he crossed the ropes half an hour ago, he was still convinced that all he needed to do was take his time. And then, blow by blow, he'd take me to pieces. It hasn't worked out like that. I keep evading his grasp, I'm always a half-step ahead of him.

He throws a monstrous left hook. It's so quick it's like a whip-lash, and I can see from the way he has put his entire bodyweight into the shot that it's carrying the force of a runaway truck. Haye might already be thirty-six, he might have lost a tiny bit of the aura he had when he was crushing every fighter that crossed his path but he's still possibly the most dangerous puncher in this division. That left hook should settle the fight. It should be the knockout blow that puts me in my place. A full stop at the end of all the vicious words we've hurled at each other over the last few months.

Instead he finds himself swiping into empty space. I jerk up, away from his flailing glove, and laugh at him. Three rounds later his Achilles snaps. He should give up. He can barely stand; his balance is fucked; whenever we come together he tumbles to the ground in an ungainly mess of arms and legs. And yet he's still snarling, still trying to damage me. It's like being in the ring with a wounded lion. His face is a mask of hurt and incredulity. Even as I'm smashing him with punch after vicious punch, I don't think he can quite believe what has happened to him.

He didn't think this was possible. Nobody thought this was possible. Except me.

David Haye thought I'd be an easy touch. He was a former undisputed cruiserweight champion of the world, the darling of the British media, and he was up against a live wire Scouse headcase who'd say anything to get attention; a firework who could go off at any minute.

Haye believed I was willing to let myself get smashed to bits in return for a fat cheque. It didn't matter that I was a world champion, fresh from blowing away Haye's friend, BJ Flores, in the first defence of my title; he was convinced our bout was going to be a walk in the park. I'd never seen anyone with that level of arrogance and cockiness – it spilled out of every pore of his body. He sweated conceit.

Even Eddie Hearn didn't think I was going to win that first bout with Haye. In Eddie's opinion, Haye was a proper heavyweight and I wasn't. Like Haye, he thought I was happy to swap a beating for a big wedge of cash.

In one respect, David and Eddie were both right: I *was* fighting for the money. Where they were wrong, very wrong, was that, deep down, I believed that I could and would win. Haye had conveniently forgotten that when I was a boy, fresh off my first ABA title, I'd kicked his arse while we were sparring. I'd been given £100 for the privilege of forcing him down on one knee. This time, I was going to be paid a lot more to do a lot worse.

To this day, I don't think David understands how I beat him. I'm not sure that he can even quite believe that I *did* beat him. He told me this recently, and I said: 'That's your problem right there.' I asked him why he never thought to put a rematch clause in.

'Tone, if somebody had told me you'd beat me, I'd have laughed in their face. You don't understand. As far as I was concerned, it couldn't happen.'

All of that meant that when I leaned in close at the first press conference, so close I could smell his breath, looked him bang in his eyes and said, 'I'm going to smash your fucking face in,' I could see him struggle to process what had just happened. I could tell he was thinking, *the cheeky bastard – he actually thinks he can beat me.* He clenched his jaw. Then I pushed him really hard on his chest. Disbelief was followed quickly by anger. You see so many things when you're in that close. I watched the precise second that Haye lost it and punched me right on the chin. He thought I was going to drop. That was his second surprise.

'What's that, you pussy? Are we punching at press conferences now?' I asked.

'We're punching at press conferences.'

'Good, I know where we stand now. Don't dare come head-to-head with me again.'

The security guards rushed in and the press went crazy. We were surrounded by noise and chaos, and it felt as if there were an explosion of camera flashes, but I was calm. I'd shown Haye that I meant business.

I'm brilliant at all the trash talk and mind games. I know that if I can embroil my opponent in a drawn-out psychological battle, then by the time we're under the lights, I'll already have gained a psychological edge. Some fighters won't play at all, no matter how hard you prod them. Usyk was like that. He acted all soft during the build-up to the fight and made a big thing of not being able to speak English. That was true, but what I realised later, and wished I'd known before, was that the fucker could definitely understand it.

It was different when I fought David Haye the first time round. The psychology of our contest was more important than just about any other element. Over the days that followed our little spat there were more press conferences, more media commitments. I saw them as a game. All I wanted to do was mess around with his mind, keep pissing him off. For him it was mental torture. I kept winding him up, tighter and tighter, playing on that big fucking elephant of an ego he has. I wanted to annoy him so much that he ended up wasting energy on that rather than thinking about the things he should have focused on. Lots of it was stupid. 'David, you've got a hairband on; I can't take you seriously.' But I knew it would get under his skin.

Maybe in the past I'd have got sucked into the drama of it all and ended up doing something stupid. People used to be able to play on my emotional vulnerabilities: I got too attached to people, too involved in situations. But my mentality was changing by then. For most fighters at the very top, whatever they might say, boxing is a business to them. Don't get me wrong, someone like Anthony Joshua is a fighter to his core, but he's been operating at such an elevated level for so long that whatever rough edges he might have had were rubbed off years ago.

Tyson Fury is the same. It's all business to him. He's acting that bravado. For a long time, I was in that minority of boxers who still operated with a street mentality. I saw the same in Dillian Whyte. That time between becoming world champion and fighting Haye was when things shifted and my priorities changed. I wasn't a street kid any more. I couldn't take things personally as I would have once upon a time because that just didn't work in the top echelons. I realised that everything had to be about business first and fighting second.

That meant that I could keep a distance, no matter what David said. I had nothing left to prove. I'd been British, Commonwealth and world champion. I was only fighting now to secure my family's future. He couldn't tick me over. What could he say? That I'd been knocked down? So had he. That I'd lost fights? Yeah, you've lost fights, too, David. I forced him to sit down and think: *How the fuck am I going to get to this fella, because he's getting to me?*

It also meant that when he announced live on TV that he was going to put me in a coma and that the next time my family saw me it would be to visit me in hospital, it didn't affect me as much as he'd obviously hoped it would. I was by myself in my hotel room at the time and to begin with, I was fucking outraged by his words. Nobody had ever gone after me like that. My head was buzzing with thoughts. *Why,* I started asking myself, *would I ever put my kids in this position?*

But then after an hour or so of sitting there thinking about it, I got my head round what he'd done. I began to see it as a source of strength. He wasn't the sort who'd usually talk about personal stuff. In bringing up my family, he'd played his final card. That was the worst he could do or say and it couldn't touch me. I knew then that he was fucked. He'd called me everything, tried to degrade me, and it hadn't worked.

That thought calmed me down. A couple of weeks later, he came to Liverpool and made a fool of himself while wearing a bizarre pair of dark glasses, calling Scousers every name under the sun, bringing up people's mothers. He was fantastic at that press conference.

At one point he shouted, 'Deep in all of your tiny minds, you know this guy is getting drilled to the canvas.' Which, it turned out, was just his warming up. He carried on: 'This right hand is going through your fucking head. All of these fucking retards know it as well.'

I found that hilarious. Mostly because it was more evidence that he'd lost it.

Still, I took Haye's threats seriously. In the days afterwards, I sat Rachael down and said, 'Listen, I could really get hurt in this fight.'

That's why, two weeks beforehand, we walked into Paul Crowley & Co. Solicitors and I drew up a will leaving everything I had to her. We weren't married at the time, so I was worried that if anything were to happen to me, she might end up in trouble. I signed my life over to her and I think that's the moment when, maybe for the first time in my career, she felt genuine fear about what might happen to me. We took the decision that she'd take the kids to Dubai while I was fighting. That was another first.

Whatever she felt, and whatever the rest of the boxing world were saying – mostly that I was going to get eaten alive – I kept my mantra going: 'I'm going to win. Trust me. I know how to beat this guy.' I was determined to try to reassure her as much as I could, so I'd tell her over and over: 'It's going to be fine. Don't worry, don't worry.'

I knew how dangerous he was. As often as I told myself that I was going to beat him, I also knew I might have to get off the floor a couple of times in the process. I knew that whatever happened, I'd find myself in a bad way. And strong as my faith was, it was also a very lonely one. You'd have struggled to find anyone who thought I could win.

But then that was the story of my career. David Haye was a brilliant fighter, far better than I ever was. He was more powerful, more explosive; when his punches land, it feels as if somebody has detonated a bomb inside your head. Everyone knew that. And everyone had also seen our bodies side by side, which was enough for a lot of people to make their minds up. It was Mr Soft against the Black Hulk. Of course he was going to kill me.

They were all missing something, though. Haye thought he would just turn up and box me out of the ring because he'd seen my fight against BJ Flores up close and drawn the wrong conclusions. I looked weak and slow and had allowed Flores to land too many punches. What looking at me didn't tell you was that I was always far harder to hit than you could have guessed, and that my gas tank was bigger than his. It didn't matter that Haye's physique was incredible, with six packs and muscles popping all over the place – I could go longer than him. And it didn't matter how I fought against Flores, I'd be taking a very different approach for Haye. I knew that if I could slowly build into the fight and drag him into the later rounds, then the bout would be there for the taking.

The other thing that they couldn't see was what was going on in our minds. They didn't understand how deeply I'd sunk my claws into Haye's psyche.

He only had five good rounds in him. I could have told you that before a single punch had been thrown. At the end of round five, I knew I had him. I'd made him miss that much that he was gassed.

'Your arse is mine. You're fucked, mate,' I told him.

In the sixth round, the bastard came out and snapped his Achilles heel.

In the build-up, I'd said, over and over, 'You'd better not quit, Dave. This fight is going to get hard, you'd better not quit.'

I swear that is the only reason he carried on. Another fighter, in another bout, against another opponent, would have seen what they'd done to themselves and said: 'That's it.' There'd be no shame in that. He couldn't walk, he couldn't balance himself. His punch was still lethal, but it's difficult to knock me out with a big right hand when you're hobbling.

It still took me another five rounds to get rid of the fucker. That was my fault. I'd been so good at making him throw and miss, but now all I wanted to do was take his chin off his face. That demonstrates what a brave man he really is – one of the most courageous fighters this country has ever seen. Fuck that, he's one of the greatest fighters ever to grace British boxing.

He wasn't fighting a prospect. I was a hard-punching world champion raining blow after blow on his face. And yet he hung on. He still thought he'd get his chance to unleash that devastating right hand.

That first fight earned me three times what I'd earned in my entire career up to that point. I couldn't care less that people were saying I'd only won because of his bust Achilles – I knew the truth. I was already a world champion and now I knew that whatever happened to me, I'd secured my family's financial future. I had what would clearly be a very lucrative rematch on the horizon. Life was good.

Months passed. I began to think about the rematch with Haye. In August 2017, I went out to work as a ringside analyst at the Mayweather vs McGregor fight in Las Vegas. And then, as I sat on the private plane that was bringing me home, I saw my mate Gary's number flashing up on my phone.

'Ashley's gone.'

'What the fuck are you on about? Ashley is on holiday in Mexico. We've just touched down.'

Gary explained that Rachael's brother Ashley had fallen from a balcony. It was an inexplicable, appalling event. It doesn't make sense that a man who, like me, was afraid of heights, would have gone up so high on a forty-foot building. I cannot believe he would have jumped. It's always felt to me like there's an important part of the story missing.

I loved Ashley. I'd grown up with him and only got closer since Rachael and I had been together. I started crying. But even as the tears flowed down my cheeks, there was a part of me that refused to believe what had happened. 'This can't be real. This must be a wind-up.' I stepped off the plane, dazed and devastated but still talking to Gary, and then I got in the car, away from the wind and noise of the runway. I could hear Rachael screaming in the background. I carried on crying all the way home. I didn't know it was possible to cry so much.

I wanted to promise Rachael that everything would be OK and yet I couldn't. Nothing was right, nothing could be right. Those months between August and May were the darkest part of my life. I'd grown up with Ashley, I'd known him since he was a baby, so I was seared with pain. But for Rachael, who was so close to Ashley that they were almost like twins, it was so much worse. The pain and stress she felt was written all over her face. Every time I looked at her, my heart bled again.

Even now, there are days when I come home and I'll look at Rachael and know that all she's thinking about is her brother. That's a heartbreaking place for both of us to be. It's devastating because I can never change what's happened. If I could do something, it'd be the best thing in the world. Knowing I'm powerless to help kills me.

My home was broken, filled with grief. Losing Ashley had torn my family to pieces. Fighting was the space I could escape into where I didn't have to think about any of those other things. I was so selfish. My wife was in tears every day and I just fucked off to Sheffield.

But even then, all I could think about was Ashley. By day, I'd work like a fucking animal in the gym, and that was enough to keep thoughts of what had happened at bay. It was different after dark. I did months of crying, weeping tears of frustration and grief and anger in my hotel room every night before I went to sleep.

A sign of how much the tension and sadness were ripping me up inside was the way that I lost it when David rang to cancel the rematch, which had been planned for December. I was so raw that I needed that fight so much. Then he called to tell me that he had an injury to his bicep and that he was really sorry. I flipped, calling him every name under the sun.

'You're a prick. Do you know what I'm going through in my life? My family is ruined. I'm training to fight you, you gobshite, and you say you've got an injury. Fuck off.' Then I slammed the phone down.

I'm glad now. If we'd fought then, when I was still all over the place, Haye would have beaten me. I'd have done something wild. I know it. I don't know what, or how, but mentally I was in no fit state to be anywhere near a boxing ring. The pressure of fight week would have done me. I'd have attacked him or a security guard or someone who had nothing at all to do with the bout. All that unprocessed, confused sadness and anger would have roared out of me, burning everything it touched. I was all over the place; the cancellation was a blessing.

As the rescheduled rematch approached in May 2018, I felt far more pressure on my shoulders than I had for our first fight. Some of that was because there was now all this history and drama. Haye vs Bellew had become a proper rivalry. It was the sort of grudge match that people couldn't take their eyes off, because they never knew what we might do next.

This time round, Haye was clearly taking me more seriously. He knew how good I was, how clever I could be and how hard I could hit. He was in incredible shape. No injuries, nothing. Even at thirty-seven, it seemed as if physically he'd returned to his absolute peak. The poster boy for British boxing was back. And if I'm going to be honest, I think a lot of fans were keen to find out if what happened last time round had been a fluke. All that translated into incredible box office numbers.

The consensus in the boxing community was that I'd been lucky. It seemed as if every fighter out there was berating me, saying that if Haye had been fit, I wouldn't have been able to live with him, that he'd destroy me in the rematch. They were doing David's talking for him. Especially since everything they said was being echoed by the major boxing journalists.

In response, I ended up heaping even more pressure on my shoulders, because I was so insistent on proving everyone wrong. The world was claiming that I'd only beaten him last time because he was fighting on one leg. *Right,* I thought, *I'll fucking show you.* I told everybody that this time, David would suffer an even more devastating defeat.

When David did surface, he seemed obsessed with retribution. He kept on saying the word 'revenge' like a kind of mantra. The dictionary definition of revenge was stamped all over the posters he'd produced for the rematch. He was absolutely consumed by it.

Luckily, I had a mantra of my own: No matter what you hit me with, you cannot hurt me. The more I repeated that, the more I came to believe it.

Despite all this tension and excitement, the last days before the rematch were much more subdued. Nothing nasty or heavy was said. The final press conference was light-hearted. Making a joke about the fact that I'd called his manager a briefcase wanker, Haye got James Buckley, who played Jay in *The Inbetweeners*, to turn up.

Still, I knew that I had to maintain the psychological assault on Haye that had disturbed him so much the year before. And he seemed equally determined to try to protect himself, however he could. Right the way through the press conference, he'd kept fucking me off, putting headphones on, ignoring what I was saying as I explained repeatedly – so that he and everyone else watching got the point – that in the last match I'd beaten him twice: mentally and physically. It was a bit of pantomime on his part, designed to show that this time he wouldn't let himself get affected by my nonsense.

So, although the little shove I gave him in the final press conference wasn't as charged with aggression and rage as the first time round, it still had a very clear purpose. I wanted him to know that I was prepared mentally. I was telling him: 'Look, I'm here, and if you're not listening to what I'm saying, you'll feel what I'm doing.'

When we sat down for 'The Gloves Are Off' on Sky, I absolutely crucified him. I went for all the things that I knew would lodge in his mind, stuff that would niggle and niggle away at him. 'David, have you had your manicure done? How's your hairband looking?'

He was working so hard to ignore me, just batting away everything I threw at him. He'd take a deep breath and look up at the sky. It was like a game for both of us – one I knew I'd win.

There's no point in just chatting shit for the sake of it. It makes no sense to challenge your opponent's fitness or their jab: you know they're fit, he knows he's fit; they're a professional boxer. You need to make him start questioning himself. Every boxer will have won fights that were close. Fights where they know that they got lucky because they'd caught their opponent at a good time or where the referee's calls were in their favour. I play on all the doubts that lurk in the minds of others and make them explain them to me. 'Why do you think you won that fight? I don't think that you won that fight. Why did your corner throw the towel in against that fighter? I thought you were still fine to fight on.' If you can get to them, you know that whether he wants to or not, he'll start asking himself: *Was I lucky? Did I deserve to win that fight?* When you sow those seeds of doubt, then he's fucked, he's absolutely fucked.

That's exactly what I did against Haye. I knew his career better than he did. I started talking about the 2004 world championships, when he lost to the Cuban gold medallist Odlanier Solís. Haye had hit Solís so hard in the first round that he was knocked out on his feet. But then Solís recovered and battered Haye into submission. Haye had his opponent at his mercy, but he lacked the killer instinct to move in and finish him off.

'You spewed it,' I told him. 'You fucking spewed it.'

Haye just looked at me as if to say: *How do know these things?* I reminded him that he'd quit against Carl Thompson. Everything was precisely calibrated to turn the screw that bit tighter each time.

In the end, he bit. I started on about his defeat against Wladimir Klitschko: 'You quit, you quit, you quit.'

Almost without thinking, he replied, 'I didn't quit.' Then he realised: 'Ah, you nearly got me.' He allowed himself a quick laugh. 'I'm going to stop talking and take another breath.'

I found out later he'd been seeing a mind quack and that they'd talked about the problems he had with me. The coach had warned him against getting into debates with me. And it had almost worked. Instead, I understood, as soon as I walked out of that room, that I'd got to him. And that meant that, once again, I'd beaten him before we'd even stepped into the ring.

As soon as Haye came out for the first round, it was clear he was thinking: *I'm going to box him. I'm going to make a fool of him.* He wanted to punish me in that rematch. He wanted to draw my agony out slowly, painfully.

That didn't happen. The plan was to take the reins early on and then just control the pace right through the fight. If I kept digging and bouncing and bobbing, I knew it would unsettle him. I never lost sight of his strengths, but nor did I forget my own. All of his physical attributes were, in my mind at least, outweighed by my mental ones. My defence was better than his – so was my boxing brain and my ability to navigate my way through a twelve-round fight. I knew that as long as I didn't let him catch me cleanly, the match was mine. He's the heaviest-handed puncher I've ever faced, the strongest man I've ever fought. So I put everything into making sure I stayed just out of his reach. As soon as the first round was over, I knew he'd lost. He knew, too. He couldn't hit me. And he was fucked, absolutely fucked. He'd prepared for the wrong fight. He thought he was turning up to a brawl, but I was playing chess.

Some nights everything clicks for you. This was one of

them. I was fighting on a level that I'd only reached maybe once before in my career. I don't think I've ever been more punch-perfect than I was that night. I didn't put a single foot wrong. Everything went to plan, everything I tried just fell into place. It's so hard to explain adequately how I felt during those moments. I was up against a world-class fighter, a man who throughout his career had devastated his opponents. And while I was surrounded by all the explosive energy and violence you'd expect, I felt calm and composed, flowing easily from one movement to the next.

It's not an out-of-body experience, because you're so in the moment. It's more that your mind and body are working together in complete unity; you can make the world move at a pace of your choosing; you can't believe that any of your punches will ever miss; you can't believe that there's anything the other guy can do that could even touch you.

When you box like that, it's the best feeling in the whole world. Nothing comes close.

I dropped him twice in the third round, then two minutes and fourteen seconds into the fifth I caught him with a beautiful left hook that left him face down on the canvas.

The second that fight ended, my thoughts turned to Ashley. He'd been there at the first fight. I'd left a ringside seat empty for him at the rematch, next to where his brother and dad were. I remember how I looked over at the space where he should have been and broke down into uncontrollable tears.

CONFIDENCE IS KEY

A boxer's mentality is his strongest weapon. Far more important than his physique. Who can get inside the other boxer's head? Who's better at hiding their vulnerabilities? It doesn't matter how good your footwork is or how much power you pack in your punch. If you can't perform when you get out there under the lights, you'll never be a contender.

So much of the mental side comes down to confidence. In boxing, confidence, and the *appearance* of confidence, are key. You have to believe in yourself and you have to do everything you possibly can to ensure that the rest of the world understands that, too. You have to make them believe that you believe, even if you're wracked by doubt or fear.

Right at the beginning of my career, I'd portray myself as being confident and outgoing. I'd portray myself as being cocky and braggadocious. I always knew I wasn't the greatest athlete, but I'd go on as if I were. I'd talk so much shit. Did I genuinely believe it? No, not really, not at the start. But a point came when I didn't have to fool myself any more. I'd proved to myself so many times that I could overcome any odds to win, that I could beat any fighter who I came up against. It meant I could shut out all the sneering voices.

This was especially important in my two bouts with Haye. I never doubted for a second I'd win and I was determined to show that, because if I'd faltered, even for a second, then the results would have been very different. I couldn't afford to show doubt or weakness to Haye, and nor could I afford to show that sort of vulnerability to myself. With so few people – nobody really – giving me a chance, I had to generate all that momentum on my own.

The way people see you determines to a large extent the way that they treat you. People trust and respect you more if you seem confident. Confident people get better jobs and enjoy better relationships. It probably shouldn't be the case, but that's the way things are. However, if you can learn to carry yourself with the boldness, if not necessarily the brashness, of a boxer, you'll find that many areas of life begin to feel a lot easier to deal with.

THE BEST LIARS IN THE WORLD

If you want to be able to project confidence, you have to feel it first. That's why boxers are the best liars in the world. We have to be. First, we have to lie to ourselves. Then, we turn round and lie through our teeth to everybody else. There's nobody, going into that first bout after a crushing defeat, who won't have a little voice in their head going: *you lost last time, you're weak, you're finished.* Nobody can know. Nobody. If anyone even senses your anxiety, then you're fucked.

I used to try to kid people into believing I was something that in reality I wasn't. It wasn't quite a lie, but it wasn't the truth, either. After my fourth pro fight, I was completely skint. My left hand had been snapped in half and I didn't have enough money to pay for the operation. I was also beginning to worry I wouldn't be able to cover our mortgage. But the story I was telling people was that I'd had four fights and knocked three fighters out and that I had it all. I was the business, the hottest prospect in UK boxing. I could carry that off when I was out and about. Then the second I walked back through the door of the house I didn't even know I could afford to live in any more, I'd feel appalling levels of stress.

I carried on because I understood the power of that kind of performance. I'd do the same in press conferences. Inside I might have been plagued with doubt, but I'd stride into the room as if I were the most confident man in the world. My message wasn't: *I hope I win.* If you'd seen me, you'd come away with only one impression: *I'm going to smash you to bits.*

There would be times when I'd make weight and although deep down I knew I was fucked – because there's just no way I should be losing ten pounds in three days – I'd sit there at the press conference and announce that

I was in the best shape of my life. Although I'd struggled like fuck to lose the last pounds, having been subsisting on a diet of ice cubes for days, and I felt dead on my feet, I'd never say that. If I did, I'd literally be able to see my opponent expanding as his confidence grew. A minute ago, he'd have been feeling like me. He might have been feeling worse than me. Now, he'd be thinking to himself: *I feel great.*

Instead, I'll tell everyone who will listen that I feel absolutely fantastic. Even as these words come out of my mouth, I know I'm talking shite, that in reality I'm at death's door. My cheekbones are drawn, my forehead will be sunken, my eyebrows sticking out, because I've drained so much fluid from my body. Yet, I'll still be telling myself and the world at large: 'I'm going to do it.' And I'll carry on kidding my bollocks off until I genuinely do believe it.

Your mind is so powerful that it can drown out every single message your poor, damaged body is screaming at you. You project that confidence because you have no choice. And the more you do project that confidence, the more you'll feel it.

The power behind this approach is that it allows you to change your mindset. If you focus on victory more than you do defeat – the things that could go right rather than wrong – then you'll instantly be thinking along more positive lines.

When you're feeling short of confidence, you don't need to bellow about it in a room full of strangers, but it'll help if you spend some time refocusing your mind. Imagine how good it'll feel when you absolutely smash the presentation you're due to give at work. Think about all the times in the past when you've enjoyed success. Reflect on the good qualities you know you possess. Individually, these might not work. Taken together, they supercharge your confidence.

SHOW, DON'T TELL

There's a feeling that I reckon only boxers know. It's sitting there at the press conferences and weigh-ins before a fight and finding yourself the subject of a scrutiny so intense that you feel as if even your bones are on show to the world. Your opponent, the media and a fucking cartload of other people have an obsessive interest in the exact current condition of both your mind and your body. It begins on the first day that news of the fight breaks; although it's pretty mild then. And then as month follows month, and week follows week, it gets more and more acute. By the time of the match itself, it's almost unbearable.

It's a weird ritual. I sometimes think that somebody watching for the first time would think they were watching two bulls fighting over a female in a nature documentary. It's so choreographed – there are rules and routines – and yet beneath all that it's about rage and power and weakness. Horrible primal emotions.

In your everyday life, people subject you to that scrutiny – that's what human beings do. They'll watch your face as you speak or the way you hold yourself as you enter the room. Most of the time, they won't even know that they're doing this, but unconsciously or not, their brains will be receiving a relentless procession of information. You're always communicating. Whether you're silent and still or jumping around full of energy, you're saying something. You can't change that. What you can try to control is the message you convey.

The difference between boxers and the average person is that we pay specific attention to the way we're perceived. As a result, we make conscious efforts to do as much as we can to control the impression we give out.

I found that the way I stood, the way I held my body, made a difference not just to how I felt, but also to how others perceived me. That was as true when I was a kid wearing a bulletproof vest on the door of a nightclub as it was for those crucial seconds I spent walking from the dressing room to the ring.

Your opponent will be watching you for any sign of weakness. You have to show him that you believe you're invincible. Don't apologise for existing – occupy that space. I project aggression, dominance, presence. It's why when I walk into a room you'll think I'm taller and bigger than I am. It makes me feel more in control of what I'm doing and it determines how people treat me: they'll listen when I speak, they'll probably be nicer, more respectful. Because

I give them the impression of somebody who knows his value, they respond to it. It's not nice, and it's not very polite sometimes, but it's true. If I acted like a loser, they'd treat me like one. It might sound as if this is a very aggressive, confrontational way of living life. Perhaps in some ways it is. But I think it's also a very good way of avoiding those sorts of situations.

I'd learned all that in Wavertree. If you can't fend off the wolves – if you can't show that you're confident and know what you're doing – the people on the streets will eat you alive. That's how they are. You've got to be one of two things in Liverpool. Either you have to know how to handle yourself in a fight or to be able to tell a joke. At some point, you'll need to rely on one of them to get you out of trouble. (To be fair, both of these things are just as likely to get you in trouble if you're not careful.) If you can't do either, then sorry, lad, but you're fucked.

When I was growing up, it was precisely because I carried myself with confidence that I didn't get picked on or pushed around. You're preparing yourself psychologically for those situations and in doing so, you're increasing the chances that you won't have to do anything violent or unpleasant. What I didn't realise until recently is that all the posturing I did in Wavertree has a basis in actual science. Taking a confident stance actually makes you feel confident. Making your mouth into the shape of a smile actually makes you feel happier. Faking it until you're making it actually works.

The confidence you need in boxing is different to other walks of life. In boxing, you need that swagger and arrogance, that willingness to climb on the ropes and scream 'I'm the fucking greatest.' That might not work so well in an office. There's a risk that if you were as brash as I used to be then you could end up alienating others. But a lot of the principles are the same. Body language is so important, so be really attentive to what the signals you give off will communicate to others. If I act stressed or anxious, I'll probably feel stressed and anxious. Everyone around me will pick up on this, probably get stressed themselves and blast those feelings back at me, which will only make me more stressed and anxious. Showing people that you're confident is just as impactful as telling them.

THE POWER OF EXPERIENCE

Part of confidence is relying on your own reactions; trusting that you'll be able to respond in the right way at the right time. By the time of the David Haye fight, I was so experienced that I was in complete control of everything I was doing and saying. There was nothing that David could say that I hadn't heard before. I was a master of winding people up. He's a clever lad, but he couldn't live with me. No matter what he said, I could bounce back immediately.

The more I went through those high-pressure situations when I needed to project confidence, the better I got at reading the room and calibrating my responses accordingly. Don't be surprised if the first time you try, you end up getting it wrong. Anybody who says it's easy is taking you for a fool. And if you don't quite nail the act first time round, don't be disheartened – keep doing it again and again until you've perfected it.

I know that in the early days, I was much more likely to lose my sense of proportion and end up saying some silly shit. Ahead of my first fight with Nathan Cleverly, I jumped up out of my seat and shouted, 'Get outside, you fucking rat.' It was my first time in the media spotlight and it shows. I wasn't used to being the focus of so much intense attention. So I didn't just overstep the mark, I fucking leaped over it.

The only reason you get better is because you learn your lessons. I went home that day and I knew I'd never make the same mistake again. I also knew that the next time would be easier. Confidence is a skill like any other: the more you practise it, the better you'll get.

THE IMPORTANCE OF FIRST IMPRESSIONS

Boxers don't get to make the ring walk twice if they fuck it up the first time. And most of the time in life you won't get second chances to make that first impression. A lot of people will have made up their minds about who and what you are before you've even opened your mouth.

I'm mixed-race – my mum is black, my dad is white – but you wouldn't necessarily be able to tell right away. That put me in a strange position, especially in the north of Liverpool, where the Rotunda was. People like me from the south of the city, which was much more diverse, always thought of that area as much whiter.

It made me realise how quick others are to form an opinion based on poisonous old prejudices they'd picked up from their parents and never questioned. For ages, everybody at the Rotunda thought I was white. A couple of times, some horrible shit came out of a fighter's mouth. I'd have my headphones on so I wouldn't hear it, and yet you could lipread easily enough. It wasn't like they were trying to hide it. I wouldn't say anything, I'd just make them pay in the boxing ring. Afterwards they'd be complaining, asking why I was giving out hidings to my teammates.

Nobody ever knew the real answer, not for a long time. I didn't feel like I could open my mouth because I worried what would happen. It wouldn't have got serious: there's no way Jimmy would have let that happen. But there are ways you can make somebody feel uncomfortable, like they don't belong.

I didn't want to risk that so I did what I could to stay away from those people. Ultimately, you just learn to live with it. That's the saddest thing. That's what you do.

People only realised after the first time my mum turned up at the gym and asked if Anthony was there. She was met with blank stares. They just said, 'There's no Anthony here.'

At the time everyone called me 'Bellew'. 'Anthony Bellew,' my mum persisted.

That was when it clicked for Jimmy and the others. It explained the velour tracksuits and loud rap music and the diamonds in my ear. It changed a bit after that, although one thing you learn quickly is that if you scratch the surface, even quite nice people can hold some surprising opinions.

There was one day when a mate who'd just got his first purse after turning pro bought himself a white gold chain. I went back with him to his house and the first thing his mum said was, 'What are you doing with a nigger's chain on?'

My mate looked at me with horror on his face, then started staring at the floor. He didn't say anything to me, what could he say? I just felt painfully uncomfortable. What made it so awkward was that I knew she was a really lovely woman, a brilliant mother.

But that was what she had ingrained in her. That prejudice had been passed on to her by her mum and dad and she'd never thought twice about it since. You see it even now. There are still some people who I look at and think, *You haven't changed your ways. You are exactly the same now.* Education's the only thing that's going to resolve that.

I hate the fact that two decades into the twenty-first century there are still so many people who will judge you on the colour of your skin, not the content of your character. But if I have learned anything from this, it's that when somebody shows you who they are, believe them. They might be racist, or a bully or a liar, it doesn't matter. They've done you a favour by revealing what they're really like. You might be able to change them, more likely you'll find it's too late. All you need to do is steer the fuck away. Your life will be far better for it.

SUMMARY

- Everyone will have moments when their confidence fails them. Imposter syndrome comes to us all at some point. But you can trick your brain. The more you tell yourself that you're going to win, the more likely you are to enjoy victory.

- People react to the version of you that they see. If you project confidence, you'll feel it yourself and other people will respond positively.

- Don't expect instant results. It took me a while before I could get the hang of all the braggadocio that goes with big-time fights. But trust that practice will help you to hone your ability to project confidence. You will get there.

- You only get one chance to make a first impression. Don't waste it.

CHAPTER 11
AFTERLIFE

Goodison Park, 29 May 2016

I start talking to myself, 'Three . . .' Then I turn to the referee, who's still counting. 'Move out of the fucking way, I'm going to kill him.'

'Four . . . five.'

'Get out of the way, let's go.'

The ref stares at me. 'You're crazy. Six . . . you're crazy . . . seven.' He grabs my hands, checks to see if I'm OK.

I'm lucky that it's Victor Loughlin, the best referee in the country. He's always had perfect timing in fights. He never stops them until the exact right moment. Someone else would have waved the fight off when they saw me roll backwards. Victor lets me get up. He stares at me closely, to check I'm solid on my feet. He knows that the fact that I'm talking to him, even if I'm being a bit of a prick, shows that I know what's going on.

'Where are you?'

'Goodison Park.'

My fitness has saved me. All that work, all that sacrifice, means that my legs are strong. I could fight twenty rounds tonight and still have energy to spare.

The bell goes. I'm still in this. There had been a moment earlier on when I thought, for fuck's sake, he's going to catch me. But although he knocked me over, I know he cannot finish me. He cannot keep me on the floor. No one, not even Mike Tyson, could keep me on the floor tonight.

For the first ten seconds after I get back to my corner, I don't hear a word Dave is saying to me. He's just a small person getting in my face. Then, suddenly, I can make out his penetrating Yorkshire voice.

'You got greedy, you got greedy.'

I know that I'm a greedy fat bastard. The last thing in the world I need right now is that little man screaming it at me. I fucking know I'm greedy. I've been a big kid all of my life. I start laughing to myself: years ago I'd been a fat boy going nowhere, and now here I am. In a fucking world title fight. It's almost too weird and hilarious to process. Then that's it. Nothing. I don't remember a single moment of the second round.

When I stand up for the third round, I've completely forgotten about the preceding minutes. This has happened before. It's the result of the toll that making weight takes on your mind and body. Losing that much of your body mass so quickly, while training like a lunatic, drains your energy and your ability to form and keep memories. Your mind just closes on you. You're fighting on natural instinct. It's like you're in aeroplane mode. The only thing I remembered from my bout against Isaac Chilemba was arriving at the arena; I don't recall a single thing from the fight itself or how

I got home, or that I went crazy in the dressing room afterwards, smashing it to pieces.

In my head, the clock is still ticking. I can't let this get past six rounds, I can't let this get past six rounds, I've got to get him. I can't let him absorb everything I have, wear me out, then slowly take me apart. I know I've been on the floor and I know that if he drops me heavily again, that could be it. I need to get in and trade with him. I need to draw him in, then counter.

I'm an underrated counter-puncher. It's my strongest weapon. I'm not naturally the strongest or the quickest fighter, but my timing is sweet. More than that, I've worked fanatically, on my fitness and on my game plan. I've studied Makabu so closely that I'm confident I can predict exactly what his next move will be. I'll know before even he does.

The moment I can tempt him into throwing that lazy right-hand jab is the moment I can smash him with my left hook. That's what we've practised over and over during the training camp. All I need is for him to slip once. The minute I feel that his gloves have gone over my shoulder and past my ear, only one thing is coming: a punch that will go right round his body, exploding into his skull from the very edges of his vision. Fuck off, I've kidded you. You're asleep and it's my night.

The third round unfolds. I hurt him numerous times. This is the pivotal moment. The trap I set is perfect. I let him bring me onto the ropes. He thinks he's got me in the corner. What he doesn't realise is that it's a trick. He comes in closer and swings a big left hand, which I block with my right and then I counter.

My right hand was powerful. I'd rendered people unconscious

with it numerous times. But the left hook was the punch I felt most comfortable throwing. I'd perfected it by studying all the great left hookers as a kid: Joe Frazier, Félix Trinidad, Mike Tyson. The short left hook I smash on his temple is the product of all that practice. It doesn't look like a hard punch, but believe you me, it's vicious. His legs shiver, he backs up at the speed of fucking light and I know I've really got him.

I chase after him and get him against the ropes. I hit him with a combination – all the shots are going in. Nothing's really catching. He's blocking most of my punches; only a few are getting through. I continue to chase him, this time to another side of the ropes. I'm on him. He brings his gloves up to his head in a defensive posture. I pull one of them down with my left hand and smash him on the temple with my right. He stumbles and although he's clearly vulnerable, I know he's still dangerous. I can see he wants to knock my head off with the same punch he used in the first round.

Then he throws a right jab. The punch I've been waiting for all night. I see it coming, then slip, moving all of my weight onto my left leg. His glove swings into the space above me where seconds before my body had been. Now. Bang! I move across and unleash my left hook.

A proper punch doesn't just come from your fist and arms. You might be able to hurt somebody that way, but you'll never send them to sleep. If you want that knockout, then the punch has to begin at the bottom of your feet before travelling right through to your hands. My left leg has been loaded with every single volt of power I possess, then I explode. Fuck off!

The second the fabric of my glove kisses his chin, I know he's not *getting up again. To make sure, I hit him with two more to the back of the head as his unconscious frame crumples to the canvas. The referee jumps in. Makabu is asleep on the floor and I look up to the clouds above the stadium and think about Jimmy Albertina. I've done it. I'm still not sure how. But I've done it. I'm world champion.*

Emotion floods my body and I drop to my knees. There's relief; there's exaltation. I've forgotten about Makabu. Tears roll down my cheeks. I think to myself: Lad, you've done it. *My whole life has been about reaching this moment.*

Then Dave is hugging me. Then I have another blackout. I remember almost nothing until the interview. Ten minutes go by where I have no recall of all the people coming up to congratulate me or the crowd going wild.

There's one memory that does stay with me. Although only minutes ago I wanted to kill Makabu, now I only have admiration and respect for him. Actually, it's more than that – it's something close to love. I go to him; check he's OK. Because, of course, what's happened to him could easily have happened to me instead.

Just over two years after my triumph at Goodison, I stepped out onto the canvas for the last time.

I'd known beforehand that I wouldn't be fighting again. For decades I'd asked so much of my body. I'd pushed it and pushed it. My will and determination had extracted more from it than I'd ever thought possible. Now, I was paying the cost. I'd carried major injuries coming into four of my last five fights. Against Usyk, it was a cracked rib that was serious enough to prevent me from sparring in the last two weeks before the fight. Like the others, it was dangerous enough that I probably shouldn't have stepped into the ring, but nobody had ever known about them, because I never wanted it to look as if I were offering up excuses. I fought through pain, I fought full of antibiotics. I knew that if I carried on like this, my body would break down completely. In that respect, retiring wasn't a hard decision. It was time to stop.

It would have been perfect to say farewell to boxing at Goodison. As it was, I prepared for my last fight in a dressing room I didn't like, which in turn was in the Manchester Arena, a venue I'd never been that keen on, either. I'd fought there a number of times, but I could never get on with it in the same way as I did The O2 or the Liverpool Echo. Perhaps it was the memory of the hand I smashed there all those years ago against Hastings Rasani. What made up for that was the fact that the crowd were amazing. The match was a sell-out; it really felt as if they'd all showed up for me – 20,000 Mancs there to see a Scouser get fucked.

I sat there going over my fight plan over and over again, and running through different scenarios in my mind. What if he does this? How will I respond if he does that? How do I adapt to him? There was no space for contemplation of what I'd been through in the last decades, or what I was about to lose. Everything was about this moment. Then Ralph, the man who'd given the final call for every single professional fight of my career, knocked on the door of the dressing room: 'Tone, time to go.'

For the first time ever, I didn't enjoy the walk to the ring. My head was full of an uncomfortable mix of sadness and anger. I was annoyed because I knew that the chance to fight for the undisputed cruiserweight title was coming at the wrong time in my career. I'd had the chance to dive straight into unification fights as soon as I became world champion, but there were other things that needed to be addressed first. Once I had that belt, everything changed. Glory didn't matter so much any more, the next part of my career was going to be all about money. I could have entered the World Super Series and hoovered up all of the other cruiserweight titles, but the two fights with David Haye earned me more than I could have got from every single bout in that tournament put together.

I had a shot at the undisputed cruiserweight title now, it would have been an incredible way to end my years in the ring, but I was facing the best boxer I'd ever come across. I'd spent my entire career being underestimated by other fighters. Now, in my last fight, I realised that I'd underestimated Usyk. I'd studied his footwork beforehand and I knew he was good, but it wasn't until I was in the ring with him that I realised how brilliant he was.

There was something so skilful about the way he positioned and moved his lead foot, fooling me into thinking he was always in range. Which of course he wasn't. What it meant was my mind could never settle or take a break.

Every single second that we were in that ring, he was making me work.

His accuracy was incredible and he also had an amazing ability to adapt and adjust, which meant he was able to frustrate me over and over. There were times when I was trying to force him to stand still while I set a trap for him, only to discover that in fact I'd blundered straight into a trap that he'd set for me. It was crazy.

Still, I felt as if I had the better of him during the opening rounds. And then, from maybe the sixth round, I could feel I was tiring too fast. It was a strange place to be. I knew I was ahead in the fight and yet there was a voice in my head going, 'Lad, you're fucked.'

He never gave me a single moment to rest or recover. I'd be watching him trying to manoeuvre me and thinking, *you sneaky bastard – I can see what you're trying to do*. Except, as I would learn quite soon, it turned out I couldn't.

As the eighth round wore on, I still thought my game plan was working. I was ahead on the cards and there were only four rounds left after this. If I could hang on and avoid being knocked out, I'd win.

The problem was that I was so tired that by this stage, I could barely breathe. When the end came, it came quickly. Usually when I fought, I'd keep my right hand up high to stop me from getting clipped by a punch coming from my blind spot. I still wanted to give myself that defence now, but I no longer had the energy to support my right hand. At the moment that the punch from Usyk hurtled round the side, out of my peripheral vision, my glove was sagging far too low. I'd thought he was looking for a shot down the middle. He'd *convinced* me he was looking for a shot down the middle. I might have been able to stop that. I couldn't do anything about the punch that swung round my glove and slammed into my head.

In truth, he'd finished me long before the eighth round. He'd finished me when he'd dragged out every last piece of energy from my body. I'd come into that fight in good shape – he *made* me tired. He'd drained me physically and mentally because, and it's hard to admit, he has a better boxing brain than me. His fight plan was better than mine and he executed it brilliantly. Although perhaps he's not a fighter who can take you out with one punch, in every other aspect he's perfect, probably the best cruiserweight ever. He grinds you down, makes you pay for every single mistake. There was no shame in losing to someone like him.

I'd been defeated. And then I found I was at peace. In the past I'd felt annihilated by every other loss, every draw. Even those wins that were that bit closer than I'd wanted them to be. Now, I was calm. I'd given everything. I was at my very best but he'd beaten me and that felt fair. Normally, I'd want to get out of the arena as quick as humanly possible. That night was different. I found I was all right. I went to the post-fight press conference – something else I'd never done before after a disappointment – and told everyone there that I'd lost to the best man. I talked about how this was the last time the world would see Tony Bellew. From now on, I was going to go back to Anthony Bellew.

There's a song I was listening to on repeat around then: 'Kill Jay-Z'. In it, Jay-Z lists all of his faults, all the bad things he's done and regrets. It resonated so much with me. I understood that desire to rid yourself of all the stupid shit you carry around on your conscience. I wished I could purge myself. I wished I could take all of it back. I wished I could wipe away all of the Tony shit and just have Anthony left. But you can't. It's all done and you have to learn to accept it.

YOU CANNOT FIGHT FOR EVER

After the first David Haye fight, Eddie Hearn had phoned me.

'The money's come in. Are you ready for it to drop? When you see your bank balance tomorrow, give me a call. You're a millionaire now, mate, you're a multimillionaire. Pay your tax, pay the VAT, look after it.'

All I could say was, 'Fucking hell.'

My first reaction when I saw the cash was sitting there was: 'Wow.' I had a huge buzz. But this was followed by a very different feeling a couple of minutes later. It didn't give me what I'd always assumed it would. I thought millions would make me happy for ever after and yet all I could think was: *I need another fight.* I saw then that it was never the money I was chasing. It was the brutal, unrepeatable thrill I got from fighting. The money was for my family, the fighting was for me.

The hardest part of retirement has been letting the fight go away, because the desire never goes. I still want, more than anything, that feeling only fighting gives me. I still think I could destroy half the clowns who are out there at the moment. By the standards of the game, I'm not even that old. And my boxing brain is probably more powerful now than it was at any stage in my career. Let me into a ring and I could make a fool of people. Journeymen, really good fighters, I don't care; I'd know how to beat them. I know the little things I'd need to do; I know what buttons to push.

Except they've got the one thing I can never get back, no matter how hard I try: youth. Their bodies can take the gruelling punishment of a twelve-week training camp followed by thirty-six minutes of violence. Mine can't.

Fighting was all I'd known for decades, so retirement felt like losing a piece of myself that I'd never get back. And yet I always came back to my body and my fear of it breaking down. I couldn't get round that. I had to let go.

A lot of people say that the hardest fight of any boxer's career is the one they have to face when they retire and I think there's a lot of truth in that. Change is always tough. It's often forced upon us when we least expect it and when we feel least willing, or able, to embrace it. But it's also an inevitable part of life, something that affects every one of us at one stage or another. When that moment arrives, you have to recognise it for what it is, accept it and move on to something new. Much as you might want to, you cannot fight for ever.

YOU'VE HAD YOUR TIME, LAD

It's so weird when I go into the arena now. I get all the same cues that used to activate all of my senses: the noises, sights and smells that told me it was time to fight. And I feel sad because I still, to this day, love fighting so much. I miss it more than I can even describe. But there's a voice in me that says: *you've had your time, lad. You've put your family through enough.* Tony Bellew is the part of me that I'm trying to draw away from, even if I'll never let it all go.

I can't stop doing commentary, because it's work, but I have made efforts to make sure that temptation doesn't end up tugging at me too much. I could still go to the gym and box without fighting, but I know that if I did that, it would lead me back into the ring. So I don't. It's a brutal solution and yet it's the only one that works.

And I don't watch my division that much any more – certainly not as much as I used to, probably not as much as I should. I still love boxing and I still love talking about boxing, but I don't ever want to *study* boxing again. I can't afford to immerse myself in the sport like I once would have. That sort of focus would only end up pushing me in a direction I don't want to go any more.

When you've put a phase of your life behind you, make the break as complete as you can. There's a reason why lots of recovering alcoholics try to avoid pubs and bars. If you don't put that distance between you and the things you used to do, they'll always be calling to you and you won't be able to make the clean start you need.

GIVE YOURSELF NEW CHALLENGES

In the beginning, I had doubts about going on SAS: *Who Dares Wins*. Mostly about the 'celebrity' element. Although I'd always embraced my role as a showman, it was only for pragmatic reasons. I did it because I knew that it was important for my career. I wasn't interested in attention for its own sake. Now I look back on it, I wish I could have fought my entire career wearing a mask, with nobody knowing who I was. I just see fame as an intrusion on your privacy.

So I didn't go on because I wanted to get more followers on Twitter or a photospread in *Hello!* magazine. I did it partly because I wanted to be pushed to my limits and find out whether or not I could have been a soldier, and partly because I knew I was in a really dark mental space and I needed something to jolt me out of it.

Before that show I wanted to kill everything. There was so much nastiness in me and for the first time in almost twenty years, I no longer had the outlet that fighting had offered me. The week before I went on that show, I'd literally chased another driver. He'd beeped his horn at me and I just thought, *fuck off*. I was raging, but I might have let it go. Then he stuck his finger up at me.

That pushed me over the edge. I didn't give a fuck that my wife and kids were in the car, and I didn't care that we were in the middle of the city centre. I accelerated and caught up with him at the next set of lights. As soon as I pulled level, I jumped out and started trying to open his car door. All the while I was screaming, 'I'm going to fucking kill you. Get out the car, you shitbag.' He looked up and I could see him shit himself as he realised exactly who I was.

As this was happening, Rachael, who was quite rightly uncomfortable with what her lunatic of a husband was doing, was shouting, 'Get in the car! Stop it.'

Still trying to wrench the door open, I shouted back, 'Fucking shut up! I'm going to kill this cunt.'

Luckily for everybody, the lights changed and he span off. If I'd got him out of the car, I *would* have killed him.

That rage was still swirling around me when I travelled out to the Scottish island of Raasay. Filming was hard. Far harder than you'd think from watching it on screen. You only see maybe a tenth of what the contestants go through; you don't see the butchery and loneliness that goes on. You cannot see the impact of sleep and food deprivation. And all the while the intensity is growing hour after hour after hour.

Ant Middleton just kept on and on at me. Right through

the show, I could sense him trying to find my vulnerable spot and I thought to myself, *it's all well and good poking the lion, but don't poke the lion too much, because you'll get a nasty bite.*

The closest I came to attacking him was the scenario with Nikki Sanderson. He made Nikki Sanderson, who is about five feet tall, pick up all seventeen stone of me. It really infuriated me that he was willing to put a young girl through so much pain. That made me want to belt him. The only reason I didn't was because he kept repeating the same thing over and over: 'Everything I do is for a reason.' And he kept saying it and saying it and I took a deep breath, realised I trusted him, and I thought, *he's using her to get to me. He's trying to break me mentally.*

He didn't break me, as it happened, but he made me open up. I hadn't anticipated that I'd be talking about my personal life, but he made me talk about things that had been going on with me. What had happened ever since Ashley and just how unhappy I was in myself. I'm for ever in his debt for doing that. I have so much respect for him.

I've never watched the show back, so I don't know what other people have seen, but I came home a completely different person.

Ant, who's by far the most positive person I've ever met, made me look at things from a different perspective. My phone became less important and I started spending half the time on it that I had in the past. I switched it off at night. Sometimes I turned it off for a whole weekend.

Instead, I paid more attention to the people around me whom I cared for most.

I also started to question what other people were doing in my life. Everyone who wasn't in my immediate family suddenly seemed less important. And I found that I could see more clearly who was adding to my existence and who was subtracting from it. Those who were hanging around me not for who I was, but for what they thought they could get from me. It's mad to think that such a little episode was able to effect such a change, but it's true.

When you've been immersed in one sort of existence for so long, it's easy to get trapped not only in particular ways of thinking about the world, but also in thinking about yourself. During those transitional phases when you're still trying to find out exactly what it is you want to do next, throw yourself into new, perhaps less friendly spaces. It's often only by leaving our comfort zone that we can learn more about ourselves.

FIND OUT WHO YOU ARE . . . AGAIN

I used to *love* trouble. I wanted it to come my way. I'd take as much of it as I could.

For a while in the nineties, Society was the hottest night-club in Liverpool. It played the best house music the city had ever seen. Just as importantly, there were three times as many women in there as there were men. You can imagine the mad pressure there was to get in and how fucked off people could get when they found themselves turned away. Dad ran the security, his best friend owned the club and occasionally I'd work the doors there.

One night when it was quieter than usual, I remember talking to a big man called Tony who used to work for my dad. I turned to him and said, 'Tony, this is boring, isn't it? Why can't we have a bit of action, something fucking going on?'

He wasn't having that at all. 'What are you on about, lad?'

'It's just boring. We stand here for three or four hours and nothing happens. Why can't it be like a bank holiday? There's always trouble then. I enjoy that. It's boss.'

'Lad, we don't want trouble. The less there is, the better a job we're doing.'

'But it's boring . . .'

'Ant, you've got nothing to prove here, mate. Honest to God.'

'I know I've got nothing to prove. You've all seen me box. I just want *action*.'

I didn't get it. I couldn't get it. I do now. I'm too scared of what might happen, too aware of what I'm capable of doing.

The last thing in the world I want these days is any trouble. I don't want any drama. I don't want to be around people who cause problems. I just want to have a nice smooth ride and enjoy all the days (and I hope there are a lot of them) I have left. If I died tomorrow, I'd die happy. I've lived a fantastic life. I've been a good example to my kids. I've left them a great head start.

All of that would have been a big surprise to the lunatic I was back then. We had to wear bulletproof vests when we worked, because the club had been shot at multiple times – by lads who couldn't get in, or people from the North End of Liverpool who wanted to cause trouble, or men who had problems with the owners. That life saw my dad get stabbed, run over in the street and put in two comas. And none of it bothered me. Not even the terrible shit my dad went through. The only thought I had in my head then was, *Who am I going to have to do if they get my dad? Who am I going to have to sort out?*

Which all goes to show that we can and do and should change.

We don't always notice even quite significant things because our lives are so full that we rarely have a moment to put our heads up and look at things properly. Retirement gave me a chance to reflect on who I was and how I was living my life.

I realised that I'd got so caught up in my own dream and all the demands that it placed on me, that I never really had time to take in the effect that boxing had on our family.

From leaving school onwards, I sacrificed everything as part of my desire to become world champion. I threw every atom of my body and mind into boxing and in the process, I lost a great deal. I was always thinking about it. I'd be planning my next fight or camp. And even when I was home, I wasn't really *at* home. I was barely present, I didn't care. When I look back now, I realise how selfish I was; at the time, of course I missed them badly, but all I was really thinking about was the fight. I wasn't willing to let anything get between me and becoming world champion.

Knowing that actually affects me more now than it did then. I feel almost a sense of disgust that I could have put fighting before my family. My children didn't ask to be born – I was the one who put them on this planet. They don't care if I'm world champion or not. My eldest lad is fifteen and he's only just beginning to play competitive football now. That's my fault. I should have been there to take him to games.

It was change that gave me the space to interrogate and reorder my priorities. What seemed essential to me ten years, five years, even two years ago, is now less significant. As time has gone on, I've lost touch with lots of the people who were important to me through my career. We've all changed. I'm never going to stop being grateful to my team, I'm proud of what we achieved together and know that although I was the only person actually going into the ring, I never felt I was alone. But I've realised that, for me, the be-all and end-all is everything that happens within the four walls of my home. What's important is what I create out of these kids and what I pass on to them.

Change can be bewildering. It can feel as if it's shaking everything in your life. But when it does happen, you should

303

see it as a welcome chance to work out what's most important to you. You might end up surprising yourself.

KEEP SETTING GOALS

Once I'd retired, I realised I'd become what I wanted to be, I'd earned what I ever wanted to earn and I'd got everything out of the sport I'd ever wanted. What was I supposed to do with my life?

I don't know if I'll ever again be gripped by a relationship as obsessive as the one I had with boxing. But I know I still have to keep setting myself goals. Even if it's little things, like golf (which I'm spending a lot more time, and far too much money, on) or just trying to make my relationship better with my wife and kids. I'm also involved in charity schemes. One that I'm particularly passionate about at the moment is called Weapons Down Gloves Up. When I was growing up, there were shootings in my area, but only serious people could get hold of guns, so deaths were few and far between. Now, however, it feels as if stabbings are becoming an epidemic. So I want to do what I can to encourage kids to think twice about doing something very stupid.

At home I want to bring up my boys to understand how lucky they are. I want to do everything I can to be happy and healthy and to maintain great relationships with my whole family. Most importantly of all, I want to do everything I can to support them in their dreams.

None of these activities will ever take over my life like boxing did, but until I do find that big new passion, they all help to give meaning and structure to it. I still get the sense that I'm learning new things, taking little steps forwards.

This book, the process of writing it, of taking myself out of my comfort zone, of trusting other people, in a world I know nothing about, has been one of those steps. Thank you for taking it with me.

SUMMARY

- Change, like failure, is a fact of life. Don't fight it – use it as another chance to grow.

- Don't look back. If you're going to make the most of change, you cannot be clinging to the past.

- When one phase of your life ends, it can be difficult to work out what to do next. Don't put too much pressure on yourself. Throw yourself into new experiences. Embrace new challenges. Learn new things.

- We can become so focused on putting one foot in front of the other that we rarely look around and ask ourselves whether we're on the right path. Change gives you this opportunity to reassess your life: make sure you take it.

- Whatever happens, no matter how much your life changes, keep setting goals.

ACKNOWLEDGEMENTS

Rachael. I said it at the beginning of this book and I'll say it at the end: it's all because of you.

Dad, all I ever wanted to do was impress you.

My boys. One day I hope you read this and understand that you were all the motivation I needed thoughout all the pain and the sacrifices.

Gary Dilsey and Fran Perry. You always believed I'd get there. I've spent many months with both of you living in apartments across the world. I hope I represented DoorSec as well as you'd hoped.

To my past coaches at Rotunda ABC. My goals wouldn't have been possible without you. That gym changed my life.

To Mick McAllister. You are a good man and a great coach. A student of the game. I'll never hear a bad word said against you and I'm so grateful for what you did for me.

To the man who changed me as a professional fighter, Dave Coldwell. You are an amazing teacher and people don't give you enough credit. I wouldn't have become world champion without you.

To Eddie Hearn. Thank you for your honesty and keeping your word. Even though I should have got a bit more on a couple of occasions (ha ha), you and your dad genuinely made me believe in boxing again after I'd been scarred. You both helped save boxing in this country.

To Albo. Jimmy, you are the greatest. I miss you and I love you. Bernie is doing great and your boys Mikey and James are both Rotunda ABC through and through. I know you'll be very proud of them.

I'll give the last word to Ashley Roberts. Your sister, your mum, your dad, Colin, Sarah, Neil, Budgie, we all miss you dearly, lad. We will never forget you and I believe you're up there now smiling at your football team and laughing at mine. You were the gentle giant with a heart of gold. I'll see you again, lad x.